YESSTORIES:

YES

IN

THEIR

OWN

WORDS

YESSTORIES:

YES

IN

THEIR

OWN

WORDS

TIM MORSE

St. Martin's Press ☙ New York

YESSTORIES: YES IN THEIR OWN WORDS. Copyright © 1996 by Tim Morse.
Printed in the United States of America. No part of this book may be used or
reproduced in any manner whatsoever without written permission except in
the case of brief quotations embodied in critical articles or reviews. For
information, address St. Martin's Press, 175 Fifth Avenue, New York, N.Y.
10010.

Design by SONGHEE KIM

Library of Congress Cataloging-in-Publication Data

Yes (Musical group)
        Yesstories   :   Yes in their own words   /   by Tim Morse.
            p.   cm.
        Includes discography and bibliographical references.
        ISBN 0-312-14453-9
        1. Yes (Musical group)   2. Rock musicians—England—Interviews.
    3. Progressive rock music—History and criticism.   I. Morse, Tim.
    II. Title.
    ML421.Y48A5   1996
    782.42166'092'2—dc20
        [B]   96-6090
                                                                      CIP
                                                                      MN

First Edition: June 1996

10   9   8   7   6   5   4   3   2   1

DEDICATED TO

YES FANS

FROM

ALL OVER

THE WORLD

WHO ARE

UNITED BY

THIS MUSIC . . .

. . . AND

TO THE UNIVERSE

WHO MAKES

ALL THINGS

POSSIBLE.

Y E S

jon anderson 1968–1980, 1983–1988, 1991–
chris squire 1968–
bill bruford 1968–1972, 1991–1992
tony kaye 1968–1971, 1983–1995
peter banks 1968–1970
steve howe 1970–1981, 1991–1992, 1995–
rick wakeman 1971–1974, 1976–1980, 1991–1992, 1995–
alan white 1972–
patrick moraz 1974–1976
trevor horn 1980–1981
geoff downes 1980–1981
trevor rabin 1983–1995

ACKNOWLEDGMENTS

I would like to thank Tanya Coad for several things. She and Sue Smith started *Relayer,* the first Yes fanzine, which has been a considerable resource for my book. As knowledgeable fans, they knew exactly what to ask the band in their interviews, instead of the usual retreading inquiries common of the press. Also, when I met up with Tanya at Yestival '94 and told her about my book, she was not only encouraging, but she agreed to the idea of me going through her Yes scrapbooks in my ravenous quest for Yes-related material. Ultimately her assistance and friendship have been invaluable to this project.

I would also like to thank Tanya's husband, Cal Reeks (who is also a huge Yes fan), for being so supportive of me and this book and for his helpful suggestions. He also endured me intruding into their lives many times, either on the phone or in person—so thanks, Cal!

Clifford Loeslin has an encyclopedic knowledge of all things Yes. At a moment's notice he can give a frighteningly complete and factual account of the band. I thank him for his assistance on my book, especially for verifying information and for giving me some great quotes.

I must say thank you to my parents, Arlene and Dick Wilson, who allowed me to type this book into their computer and have regretted it ever since! Seriously, they have been overwhelmingly patient and generous with me and this project. My sister Kirsti Fong has provided important computer assistance to me and I thank her. Also, my editor Greg Cohn and everyone at St. Martin's Press have provided invaluable help in getting the dream of having this book published to become a reality.

The following group of people I am severely indebted to (I think I owe them all a firstborn child . . .) for helping to set up interviews with the band: Christine Holz, Lisa Mikita, Tiffany Gobel and Karey Fisher (from East End), Gary Davis (The Other Road), Jolyon Burnham (Huge and Jolly), Chuck Turner, Melissa Squire, Nic Caciappo, Mike Tiano, Clifford Loeslin, and Tanya Coad.

Lastly, I want to thank Jon Anderson, Chris Squire, Bill Bruford, Tony Kaye, Peter Banks, Eddie Offord, Steve Howe, Rick Wakeman, Alan White, Patrick Moraz, Geoff Downes, Trevor Horn, and Trevor Rabin for twenty-five years of some of the most inspiring music of all time. I am especially grateful to those who submitted to interviews with me.*

*Unfortunately Jon Anderson, Rick Wakeman, Tony Kaye, and Trevor Horn were not available to be interviewed for this book.

C O N T E N T S

INTRODUCTION

In the spring of 1976, I was innocently introduced to the wonders of Yes music. A friend of mine in art class who knew I was a guitarist told me about this fantastic guitar player named Steve Howe. He didn't have to tell me much to get my enthusiasm going and into the record store to purchase my first Yes album, *Relayer*. I remember getting it home, being impressed with the artwork, putting it on the turntable, and then immediately being perplexed by this music. I could hear the guitarist was technically good, but he and the rest of this rather strange band were playing very bizarre, completely "out there" music. And what was this high-pitched singer going on about? His lyrics seemed to be the most random, abstract words thrown together in some kind of jumble. A member of my family remarked that it sounded "terrible" and I was not inclined to disagree. Yet . . . this music was unlike anything I'd ever heard before and I felt myself drawn to listen to it again. And magically I found something I liked and so I listened to it again . . . well, I think you get the picture.

Very quickly, *Relayer* was the only thing I listened to and I found I was infected with the "Yes thing." I bought all of their releases and would expound on the wonders of this band to any potential (or nonpotential) converts. So in a way this book began in 1976.

The only book about the band, *Yes: The Authorized Biography* by Dan Hedges, came out in 1981 and I have waited years for someone to update the information found in it. In 1994 I finally decided to stop waiting for someone else to do it and write the book myself. I knew that the focus of the book would be the music and that the people who are best qualified to speak about it were the band themselves. I have since spent my time on this labor of love poring over interviews and articles, transcribing radio and videotapes and interviewing present and former members of Yes. I hope you enjoy my effort. . . .

Tim Morse
Spring 1996

chapter 1

BEGINNINGS: "WE ADVANCE, WE RETRACE OUR STORY"

The beginning of Yes starts with the first musical efforts of ten English lads, as well as one from South Africa and another from Switzerland: all of whom picked up their respective instruments at young ages and never looked back.

ON MUSICAL BEGINNINGS

chris (1987): I spent all my childhood in Church of England choirs. I ended up singing in the Guilford Cathedral and eventually the St. Paul's choir. I was a six-days-a-week, in-the-church guy in the best church choir in England. So I had an early knowledge of the power of the music and singing. Then, when that phase of my life changed, I went to a regular school. I was sixteen, the Beatles had started, and I was a follower of that. I became totally absorbed in the idea of bands, electric guitars, and stuff. But as soon as I started formulating bands with friends, obviously my knowledge of church music and harmonies entered into it. Prior to that, despite having all that musical knowledge, I never played any instrument at all. Although I used to sneak into the church or the cathedral when it was closed and start up the organ—just blow everything away for a couple of hours. I couldn't really play, but I could jive around a bit—make sounds. I don't know what God thought of it, but it was pretty weird stuff. Then when I was around sixteen, I got a suggestion from a good friend of mine at school who was already a good guitarist and a pretty hip guy as well. He said to me that since I was kind of tall and had big hands, I should get a bass guitar. So I did and that is how I started playing.

I went to work for a year at a music store in London as an assistant. It was during that period that I went to see the Who, and John Entwistle was in fact the first guy I ever saw playing a Rickenbacker. Through my position in the store, I actually persuaded my boss to start importing Rickenbackers—and they did. Part of the deal was that I got one at the factory price. I've had that bass ever since and they went on to make a lot of money! (GW)*

jon (1989): Me and my brother Tony did a milk round for a local farmer, only we had to go to the field, catch the cows, and milk them first. That's when we started singing together, Everlys, Buddy Holly. When I was ten I played washboard in the Little Jon Skiffle Group and a bit later Tony dragged me into the Warriors. (Q)

(1971): In the Warriors we used to copy the Beatles. I used to go on stage thinking, "I'm Paul McCartney. I'm going to sing 'I'm Down.'" And I used to scream it out. I enjoyed the idea of the girls and the traveling. There was a bit of escapism, I think. (SOY)

bill (1991): My sister had a boyfriend when I was about ten and she must have been about fifteen or sixteen. And he gave her some brushes and said, "If you play them on the back of an album sleeve"—which used to be made of thick white card—"it sounds just like a drum." So she passed them on to me and said, "Play these, they sound just like a drum on the back." So I learned to play the brushes first, then I got a pair of sticks, then I got a practice pad, then I got a drum, then I got two drums. . . . Now I understand kids buy seventeen drums at once. (YY)

(1978): I came to London and wanted a gig. I was prepared to be in any band that had a Transit van that would go up the motorway. I was in love with the whole idea of being a musician. I wanted to be in a real group rather than a local group and play pubs. I came to London and Savoy Brown was the first audition I went to. It was the blues. I said, "I can handle that, it's no problem." They already had a drummer, but I told them they had the wrong guy. After three nights it was pretty clear I wasn't suitable so they asked me to leave. (TP)

tony (1991): My grandmother had a piano and she was a pianist. And she sat me down at the piano and that was it. (YY)

Until I was seventeen I wanted to be a classical pianist, but I started getting interested in other forms of music at school. A buddy was a trad jazz fan, and another had a collection of modern jazz records. We formed a sort of Temperance Seven Band at grammar school. I was carrying on with classical

*Please see page 157 for an explanation of source abbreviations.

music, but listening to more exciting forms. Modern jazz seemed very exciting and I liked the big bands—Basie and Ellington. In fact I joined a big band in Leicester when I was fifteen—the Danny Rogers Orchestra.

After I left art college I saw an ad in the *Melody Maker* and went for an audition with a group called the Federals. They were backing Roy Orbison on tour and in two hours I learned the entire Roy Orbison chart and went on the road. They were a good band, but into the comic showband thing. At this time I used to go to the Marquee and watch Graham Bond, Ginger Baker, and Jack Bruce. Bond was mind-shattering. I liked the sound he got from the organ. I had been playing my Vox like a piano. Actually it wasn't until six months after joining Yes that I got a Hammond. (MM)

peter (1994): Lonnie Donnegan was the first person who really turned me on to music. Basically the premise of skiffle was that anyone could play it. You had to know three chords, a maximum of five. It was a steal of southern blues with a bit of Huddie Ledbetter and a bit of Woody Guthrie thrown in to keep the white folks happy. And this guy Lonnie Donnegan was successful and had a number one record. My parents would buy these records for me and I would play these things like crazy. I got started playing guitar at a very young age, I was about seven or eight. I got a very cheap guitar my parents bought me, it probably cost about five pounds, ten pounds. And I would practice all the time. I spent most of my time until my early teens listening to these records and learning to play, instead of hanging out with the other kids. I joined my first band at sixteen and went on from there. (TMI)

steve (1992): I consider myself a natural player because there had always been something naturally driving me, ever since I was twelve. Not being a very studious child I had to work at it even harder—there were no tuition books available apart from chord books and there were no rock guitar teachers around who I could communicate with. In the sixties I was known as a pretty hot session player, but I also played in four different bands—the Syndicats, the In Crowd, Tomorrow, and Bodast. After Bodast I was P. P. Arnold's guitarist for a tour supporting Delaney and Bonnie, who had Clapton playing with them at the time. That gave me a great shove because I saw that it was possible to make it and rise above the club and ballroom circuit. I realized what I needed was a vehicle in which to express my playing, then fortunately Yes came along. (GTM)

(1987): I'd always wanted to have my own guitar style, but other people said I had one before I was aware of it. . . . In 1968 I was in a band called Tomorrow when I realized there were things I did that other guitarists didn't do. I've always enjoyed not using ordinary guitar licks, for instance. For a long time people played blues guitar. Although I like playing blues guitar, you don't hear me playing many blues phrases. In some ways it's a question of finding the most obvious things I play and then digging in around them to be more unusual and more original. I'm not limited to just one instrument. I've played a bit of mandolin, the koto, and some steel guitar, because the guitar isn't always enough for me. I also use them because I may not have found the right guitar part. When you don't know what to do, sometimes it's easier just to do something completely different. (G)

rick (1974): My earliest memory of the piano was probably from when I was about four years old. I saw my dad playing and of course I wanted to play piano like daddy. (YY)

(1981): I started when I was five, with piano lessons. I took lessons until I was eighteen, then I went to the Royal College of Music in London for two years. I did session work for people like David Bowie, Cat Stevens, and about two thousand other sessions (literally) between the ages eighteen and twenty-one. Then I got the chance to join the Strawbs, for $50 a week. They were a folk group at the time, but I loved playing in front of an audience. (MR)

(1989): I left college a year before completing my course to get my degree. And it was a gamble when you look back on it, but it was one that I had to take. I had started doing sessions, playing for different people, and I was interested in the new electronic instruments that were coming out, although there was really only things like the Mini-Moog and the Mellotron available. But I was desperate to improve the relationship of the keyboard within a band, because before it was always the organ that rarely got heard anyway. And I thought there was a tremendous future for it. . . . I was very aware that the course of musical history was not going to be changed by me, but I could be part of it if I wanted to be. (ITS)

alan (1989): I studied the piano first when I was six. My uncle was a drummer and when he noticed me pounding on the keys, he suggested to my mother that I should have a drum kit, so I got a kit for my twelfth birthday. Drums were a natural progression for me; I always felt comfortable when I sat down at the kit. (WS)

(1995): I was on the stage within three months of getting my first kit. At that time I joined a band called the Downbeats. Basically we did a lot of Beatles, copy stuff with some original material. I think the best place to learn is on stage. It makes demands of you and you really start creating. I was in that band two years and they changed their name to the Blue Chips and we won a bunch of competitions nationwide in England. We got a record contract, but I went to college. I was there about two years and the principal of the college said, "You're making more money doing this than I am being a principal. You should be a musician." So I quit and have been a musician ever since. (TMI)

(1991): I got a telephone call and someone said, "John's on the phone for you," and I said, "I don't know any Johns." And it was a telephone call from John Lennon. I thought it was a hoax initially, but he'd seen me somewhere and he said, "I'd like you to do a gig with myself the day after tomorrow." I said, "I think we have a gig, but I'll see what I can do!" I turned up at the V.I.P. lounge in Heathrow airport and there was Eric Clapton, John, Yoko, and Klaus Voormann. We literally rehearsed on the airplane, John and Eric playing acoustic guitars and me with a pair of drumsticks on the back of an airplane seat. All of a sudden we were being picked up in Toronto and taken straight to the gig and on stage. Me being young and naive to that big star kind of thing . . . I didn't realize what I'd just been through. Playing on stage with Eric Clapton and John Lennon in front of all those people was the biggest break in my career. (YY)

patrick (1995): I started on violin when I was three and a half years old . . . and I started the piano when I was four and a half. It took six months to realize that this is really the instrument I wanted to play. Intuitively, I felt I was mechanically made for the keyboard instrument, rather than the violin or stringed instrument. (TMI)

(1974): My first professional band was called Mainhorse. The other people in the band were Jean Ristori, a guitar player, and a very heavy English drummer, but the type of music we were doing at that point was just representative of the progressive music that was happening at the time. I guess you could call it orchestral rock. After Mainhorse broke up in 1972, Jean and I did a tour of Japan with a Brazilian dance company that played heavily rhythm-oriented folk music. I had been interested in Brazilian music for some time, so I was familiar with the way that type of music had to be phrased and accented. After the tour ended I went back to Europe to work on film scores. I wrote over thirty scores during this period! There was nothing much happening musically in Switzerland so I got together with Lee Jackson and Brian Davidson (both of the Nice) to form Refugee.

(1991): Refugee had management problems, and a record company that didn't understand where we wanted to be, that pushed us toward more commercial things. At one point, they wanted to bill us in America as the new Nice! Unfortunately, Brian and Lee did not have the spiritual sense to rebuild something as valiant as they had had before, so after we did our album I realized that the band was not essential, and that I would rather suffer awhile and start all over again to rebuild something that was essential. (K)

geoff (1980): I studied classical music early on, but I didn't really get interested in pursuing music as a career until I was thirteen or fourteen years old, when rock 'n' roll caught my ear. My hero at that point was Keith Emerson. He was the archetypical rock keyboard player. He was the first virtuoso keyboard player in rock. I was in a trio that played a lot of material that Emerson did with the Nice. We used to play around the north of England. After college I moved to London. I somehow managed to get into playing sessions there, and over the period of three or four years I gradually accelerated the number of sessions I was doing so that I used to turn some of them down because I didn't have time to do them all. I hooked up with Trevor Horn, who was doing freelance production at the time. We'd stay up late and go over the budget just experimenting with all sorts of gadgets, but we developed a sound that got a lot of people record deals. A lot of the compliments that people got were on the strength of the things that Trevor and I did, so we thought it might be time for us to try to do something on our own. That's how the Buggles got started. (K)

trevor horn (1981): I used to play double bass in the youth orchestra. I was playing classical music with them for about four years in the north of England. Well, my father was a musician—a double bass player in a dance band. I sort of drifted into it playing in the school orchestra, and then in the youth orchestra. And then I started to play the bass guitar in a group and I started doing it for a living. Then I came down to London and got involved in session work. I was basically just a bass guitar player. I built a recording studio with an older guy, and I started to produce records. But I didn't know I was producing records at the time. What I used to do is organize local musicians and I'd write the song. And sometimes I'd sing it and do the arrangement. Then somebody told me, "Hey, what you're doing is producing records." I never knew that. (R)

trevor rabin (1991): I come from a family of musicians. My mother is a piano teacher, my father was the lead violinist of the Johannesburg symphony for twelve years, and my brother was winning every classic music competition in sight from the age of seven on violin, and my sister is a classically trained ballet teacher and she's a great pianist. . . . So I come from a kind of pretty talented family.

I've played piano since I was six. Guitar was something I picked up on my own along the way. . . . From the piano I taught myself guitar. I've never had a guitar lesson in my life. (YY)

(1985): I was in a band called Rabbitt on Capricorn Records. It was kind of a jazz-rock sort of thing, meshed in with a lot of ballads . . . a weird combination. It was very successful in South Africa and Japan. In 1978 I left South Africa and went to England. I was producing a lot in Italy, Milan, and Germany. And then I signed up with Chrysalis Records and did the first album, which is just called Trevor Rabin. And they were very excited, it entered the charts and they wanted me to tour. But I didn't have visas and things, so I didn't tour. I did all the instruments on the first record, but there was a drummer who played on a few of the tracks. Then I did the second album where I played everything as well. I just brought a few people in to add one or two things. But then the third album (called *Wolf*), which wasn't released in the U.S. because it was the last album for that record deal, was by far the best album. It was better than the first two albums put together. (R)

ON EARLY INFLUENCES

chris (1987): I started off by just learning Paul McCartney and Bill Wyman. I just watched what they did and copied it. . . . Like the Stones, I was from London, so they were really more my bag than the Beatles. And I used to think what he was doing was just great—things like "Come On," "I Wanna Be Your Man," and all that stuff. And it was really mixed loud too, so you could really hear the bass for the first time. Then, of course, Jack Bruce too. His style was low-mid and he would usually like quite a lot of Marshall amp distortion—almost verging on fuzzbox. (GW)

peter (1991): A guy that influenced me was the guy who used to play with the Nice, Davey O'List. He was an extremely chaotic, anarchic guitar player, who would play either very, very well or very, very badly. I liked his approach, but whatever happened to him, I have no idea. (YHS)

(1994): I was always influenced by Pete Townshend. I still regard him as one of the best rhythm guitar players ever. I liked his whole attitude on stage. I remember at one of the first Yes gigs when we were taking a break in-between sets that somebody hit me 'round the back of the head. I was just about to hit the person back and discovered that it was Pete Townshend! He came up to me and said, "You're a fucking great guitar player!" (TMI)

alan (1994): The first people I started listening to were a complete wide mixture as it is nowadays. I listened to the Beach Boys and the Beatles. We played a lot of Beatle songs in the band I was in at the time. Gene Krupa and Buddy Rich were my drumming influences . . . those were the guys I listened to. My uncle was also a drummer and he kind of spurred me on to that. (TMI)

patrick (1995): Jimi Hendrix is one of my biggest influences in music in general, in the way he treated the guitar. John Coltrane, Bud Powell, Charlie Parker, Stravinsky, Mozart, Beethoven, Chopin, Frank Zappa, and of course Keith Jarrett [have all influenced me]. Miles Davis, of course, a major influence. I have always loved his music and performances, even the ones which have been condemned by society so to speak. (TMI)

steve (1976): Even before I wanted to play the guitar, I was listening to Les Paul and Frank Beecher (Bill Haley's guitarist). We had them on old 78s and I was first attracted to the pure electric guitar sound. When the Shadows first came along my brother would listen to them and say, "It doesn't do anything. It's not very emotional. Listen to Barney Kessel." My brother played clarinet, and was into traditional and modern jazz, so this was a bit hard to take—the Shadows and Barney Kessel—though I have to admit that I found Barney Kessel much more interesting. It was a very funny time. After I'd had the guitar for a couple of years, I felt that I really wanted to play well. Yet I'd hear Django Reinhardt records and I really couldn't get it into perspective. Did I have the ambition to become a great guitarist or was I just going to sit at home and play for my own amusement? (BRG)

Chet Atkins was a tremendous influence on me, I even bought one of his albums called *Teensville*, where he started off with some great rock and roll and doing blues-feel ballads. What was coming through was Chet and music, instead of some particular category of music. Anyway, I usually go through cycles in my listening habits. I tend to listen and relisten to all my records. One that always stands out is Charlie Christian, who is an exciting kind of guitarist in playing be-bop music as only he could. But mainly at home I listen to Julian Bream, whom I find has opened up a lot for me, mostly in the way of the music he's dug out and he also has a way of putting it over with guitar and orchestra . . . the ultimate thing with Julian Bream is that I like everything he does as soon as the record starts. (GP)

trevor rabin (1995): I really appreciated classical composers at an early age. The one that I started off loving and has continued to be my favorite—is almost the clichéd favorite of people who aren't into music— Tchaikovsky. But there's tons of composers that I love. Schoenberg, what I like about him is that he takes traditional musical values . . . harmonies, contrapuntal things, and kind of infests them with his twelve-tone thing. John McLaughlin and the Mahavishnu Orchestra was a big influence on me and that whole genre of music with people like Chick Corea. Hendrix was an amazing experience for me. People say he was this great guitarist, but beyond that to me his lyrics, demeanor, production, and his voice all had so much passion. (TMI)

bill (1994): I grew up with jazz. Grew up through the sixties in England with all the great American jazz drummers. We used to import albums from the Riverside label in California. I grew up therefore with Charlie Persip and

Max Roach and all the big drummers—Art Blakey, Philly Joe Jones, and so forth. That's where I learned my drums. Then the Beatles came and the Rolling Stones and we listened to those albums, but we didn't like those albums as much as we liked Monk. (S)

I suppose the Beatles were the unifying factor (of Yes). Of course we have the Beatles to thank for everything, because they proved it could be possible somehow to make crazy music and do your own artwork and to be successful. So everything we did really was inspired by the Beatles in the first place, but we eventually outgrew it. (TMI)

On the Beginnings of Yes

The seeds of Yes were planted in a chance meeting between Jon Anderson and Chris Squire at the La Chasse Club in London, where Jon had been working. The two discovered that they agreed in their musical ideals, especially in the idea of forming a band that was extremely strong vocally and instrumentally. Squire's band, Mabel Greer's Toyshop, was winding down and so they started to put together what was to be the first Yes lineup: Jon Anderson (lead vocals), Chris Squire (bass guitar and vocals), Bill Bruford (drums), Tony Kaye (keyboards), and Peter Banks (guitar and vocals). The group proceeded to live in poverty and play some of the worst gigs known to man, hoping that it would pay off someday. . . .

chris (1992): [Meeting Jon for the first time] was nothing special. This guy Jack Barry introduced us. We wound up sitting at a bar, having a beer and we just started talking about Simon and Garfunkel, I think. At the time, I didn't know that it was going to be any different than meeting anyone else. (YM)

peter (1994): I was a big fan of the Who and I liked very short names. In fact instead of the Who I always thought it should just be Who. Because you don't say the Yes. And when you had posters and people would put up fliers of who was playing, the less letters you had in your name the bigger the name could be printed. If it was three letters it could be printed very big! (TMI)

(1991): It was actually when I was in Mabel Greer's Toyshop that I came up with the name Yes, and everybody said, ''That's a bit silly.'' And Mabel Greer's Toyshop wasn't a silly name, right? (WS)

(1994): [The original Yes logo] was a simple idea, really. It just seemed like a logical thing to have Yes in a kind of balloon coming out of somebody's mouth. Simple, but brilliant! (TMI)

jon (1994): We got Tony Kaye, a very groovy guy. I had met Tony four years before in Leicester. So we sort of knew each other and Pete Banks was there. And he was already with Chris in a band called Mabel Greer's Toyshop. So the first thing I said to Chris was, ''Maybe we should change the name!'' (ITS)

Bill Bruford was advertising in the *Melody Maker*. Me and Chris rang him and said, ''You play drums?'' And he said, ''Yeah, I'm a good drummer.'' So the only way we knew if he was a good drummer was if he had a Ludwig kit. So we said, "Do you play Ludwig?" and he said, "Of course I do!" And I think what he did is quickly sprayed his Sonor kit black to look like a Ludwig. So when it came time to do an audition it looked like a Ludwig kit. But he was a good player. (ITS)

chris (1987): We had an offer to play a Saturday night booze-up at some college [the Rachel McMillan College in Deptford], so we rang Bill up. We weren't really a band at that point, but we went down there anyway and did a couple of twelve-bar blues things—a slow one and a fast one—and finished up with "Midnight Hour." That was essentially Yes's first gig. (GW)

tony (1994): At the beginning we did covers of other people's songs like the Beatles thing, the Buffalo Springfield thing, a couple of others like "America," that kind of stuff. And we just put it into a different musical ball park and embellished it and made it more symphonic and more instrumental. Although the first two albums didn't really reflect what was coming, it was the start of the way we were thinking. (ITS)

(1985): Yes was a funny band from the beginning, because it was an emotional band . . . the band didn't really come from a classical source; it only went in that direction with Wakeman. In the beginning we were very much a pop band, trying to do something different. We were always concerned with arrangements; they were our trademark. We'd take other people's numbers and just mess them around. How could you take a Richie Havens number or a Beatles number, stretch it out to fifteen minutes, and make it sound interesting? That's how we developed a following, by doing all that stuff at the Marquee Club.

bill (1982): When the whole thing started really was in 1968–69, there was a big explosion of musicians entering the so-called rock field at that time, post–*Sgt. Pepper*. It was felt after *Sgt. Pepper* anybody could do anything in music. And it seemed the wilder the idea musically the better, but it had just better work. Everything seemed up for grabs. (BB)

peter (1991): It was like doing a permanent hobby, and you actually got paid for it. It was a good time, certainly the whole London scene was a good thing, and it seemed like it would go on forever. (YHS)

jon (1994): There was definitely a feeling that we were all experimenting. It was a very, very great time in London for experimenting around '68–'69. Five major bands that came out of that time were King Crimson, ELP, Yes, Zeppelin, and Deep Purple. . . . Everybody was setting the theater for the seventies. (ITS)

bill (1994): I don't remember a whole lot of sex, drugs, and rock 'n' roll, really. I'm always one of these guys who never notices. I hated rooming with anybody. Sometimes I had to room with Tony Kaye and that was awful. At the end of the whole day of working with people you want some privacy. We used to drink an awful lot of alcohol. There was a club here in London called the Speakeasy that the band's manager [Roy Flynn] was managing as well. The Speakeasy stayed open late, until two or three in the morning. So you could pretty much play a gig in England within a hundred-and-fifty-mile radius and still make it back to the Speakeasy at about two o'clock. And we'd drink huge amounts of Scotch and Coke, which is a ghastly sweet drink. . . . And now people don't drink nearly as much, for good reason. We're all a little wiser.

I do remember the whole thing as being very argumentative, hot-blooded . . . a permanent state of friction between Jon and Chris, Chris and me, me and Jon. A permanent state of argument, really. We were from totally different social backgrounds. This is what is very hard for an American to understand, but we could have been five guys from Mars. I mean I'd never met anyone like Jon Anderson in my life! I couldn't understand physically what he was saying, he has a very strange accent from the north of England. He speaks in strange sentences that nobody can understand. It was chaos. . . .

It was a very exciting time. Time was just going very, very fast. We just lived for the band. We all lived in the same house, or most of us did. And as far as I can make out we were confined to the property, because at twenty-four hours' notice we'd have to do a gig somewhere. So you couldn't leave the building for more than twelve hours in case a gig came through. . . . We used to be like firemen, living in a firehouse . . . with a greasy pole and when the bell rang you did a concert. (TMI)

Bill Bruford, hard at play.

THE MUSIC:

"THE MUSIC DANCE AND SING"

YES
RELEASED AUGUST 1969
(U.S. RELEASE NOVEMBER 1969)

A year of hard work and perseverance began to pay off for the band with the release of their first album. It was recorded quickly, under less than ideal conditions, yet managed to capture some of the trademarks of the fledgling Yes sound: Squire's melodic and forceful bass work, Bruford's unique drumming style, Kaye's swirling organ sound, and of course the Yes harmonies. Yes didn't much care for the album after its release, but hindsight now reveals its many strengths. The record had some positive critical response at the time, but it died a quick death commercially.

Jon (1982): The band was doing really well in London, getting a real good name for itself. It toured England twice. We were ready to do some recording. We didn't know very much at that time about getting the right

An early shot of Yes.
PHOTO BY BARRIE WENTZELL/REPFOTO

engineer/producer, so we went and just recorded for about three or four weeks. . . . At that time, there was an internal decision that we wouldn't specifically try for singles. There were enough people doing that. We wanted to formulate some style of music, and package it as an album. That gives you a better chance of staying around. (RR)

peter (1991): It was kind of the blind leading the blind, because Paul Clay had never produced a band before; he had done film soundtracks. I think it was Atlantic's idea to have him. We spent about two or three days just trying to get a Hammond organ sound. Tony didn't own a Hammond at the time, he had a Vox Continental literally disguised as a Hammond. We used to put wood around it to hide its weedy stand. We did the album in about a week and probably mixed in a day and some of the songs sound like it! (YHS)

bill (1994): I was a complete novice and I didn't understand what you could do in a recording studio. For example I remember clearly on the first LP that it wasn't until we were finished making the record that I understood that you could alter the level of the instruments in your headphone balance. . . . I played the whole of the first LP with a very loud Peter Banks guitar in one ear and nothing else in the other ear and I thought that was what you got. . . . It's lovely the way people learn these things, isn't it? (TMI)

peter (1994): The engineer was a guy, I think his name was Gerald. I think we called him the Ferret or the Weasel. He was a little guy with glasses, he looked like a rocket scientist from the 1950s. He just didn't like rock music. I remember he was always asking me to turn [the volume] down. It was a little disappointing, because here we are making our own album and we were getting an engineer [saying] "Turn it down, turn it down." We were a very loud band. (TMI)

"BEYOND AND BEFORE"

chris (1995): Clive Bailey and I wrote that song in Mabel Greer's Toyshop. I think we both wrote the lyrics as well, it was one of those acid rock kind of songs. Psychedelic lyrics. I don't know if we ever really played it in concert much. I'm sure we did in the beginning of Yes, but once we recorded it I don't really remember us playing it. (TMI)

peter (1994): That was the one song that had been done before Yes were even born.... We used to start the set off with it in Mabel Greer's Toyshop and I believe in early Yes days we used to start our set off with the tune. It kind of evolved. It got bigger and bigger and longer and longer. It was kind of psychedelic. Who knows what those lyrics are about? I have no idea and I used to have to sing them. We used to sing them in a three-part harmony and this was even before Yes that we were doing this. I could still play that song even now, but I certainly wouldn't! I probably have played it more times than any other song I would imagine. (TMI)

"I SEE YOU"

peter (1994): That was a bit of a strange one. I used to get into a lot of trouble for that particular tune, because sometimes on a given night the guitar solo was so long that everybody else would leave the stage. And I'd just be up there and Bill would be playing drums, but sometimes even he would leave. It was a very free-form thing, it was never planned. When it worked it worked very well and on some nights it was a complete disaster. But I never wanted to work it out, I was always under pressure from the other guys, "Can you make it shorter . . . can you do this and that." And I was young and headstrong and I said, "No, I want to do it my way." I would end the solo by throwing the guitar up in the air and banging it on the floor. It was a very therapeutic piece for me, although maybe not for the audience. I used to get a lot of aggression out of my system in this one piece. The recorded version at the time I thought was terrible. I must admit I haven't heard it for a while, but the last time I did listen to it all I could hear was mistakes. (TMI)

bill (1995): [On the guitar solo] I think we are slightly embarrassed about it now. It's okay, but we were kids back then. (TMI)

"YESTERDAY AND TODAY"

peter (1994): We did that at a different studio, Trident Studio. It's a bit unusual because Bill played vibes on it. And I remember having a bit of a laugh because Bill said, "Oh I can play vibes." So we hired this set of vibes, but when he went to play this thing he was very nervous about it. It's a nice little tune. I wrote some of that, but I can't remember what exactly my contribution was. (TMI)

"LOOKING AROUND"

peter (1994): There are strange changes on it. . . . We had trouble with the pitching on that. We could never figure out what key it was in. (TMI)

chris (1995): That's definitely one of my favorites from the first record. (TMI)

"HAROLD LAND"

bill (1994): "Harold Land" was so-called because of a jazz tenor saxophone player named Harold Land. I came up with the name and the lyric came out of that, but it gives you a clue as to how much I thought Yes was going to be a jazz group. I was obviously a jazz head at the time, I didn't understand anything about rock at all. (TMI)

peter (1994): That was a weird one as well. I remember that was a pain to record. We had problems getting it to sound right. (TMI)

"EVERY LITTLE THING"

chris (1984): When we were in New York a couple of weeks ago, I turned on the hotel radio, when we got back from Madison Square Garden, to help me wind down. It was right in the middle of some guitar passage, and I didn't actually know what it was. I was listening to the sound of the guitar, bass, and drums, thinking "This sounds really good." I didn't realize who it was until the next line when Jon Anderson's voice came in "When I'm walking beside her . . ." It was us! . . . I listened to the rest of the track and was amazed at how good it sounded. It had quite a lot of magic about it. We obviously did something right. (C)

peter (1994): I think it was mine or Jon's idea to do that song. I always liked that. I was a big Beatles fan anyway. I think we all were. I have no idea how the arrangement came out of that. That was another one that was good live and the recorded version is representative of how the band sounded. It always went down well live, it used to wake people up. It was a happening song. The Beatles version is a playful, sing-along thing. Although the way we did it, we kind of charged into it like a herd of elephants. I don't know what that came out of, I would imagine the feel for that probably came from Bill. And that used to get faster and faster. [We played it] live at a ridiculous speed. (TMI)

"SWEETNESS"

peter (1994): It was very much Jon's tune. I don't think any of us particularly liked it. It came out as our first single and it's probably the most unrepresentative thing that could have been brought out. (TMI)

peter (1994): I would say that was a band composition. I think every-one pitched ideas in on that one. I contributed to the introduction. I think we had quite a lot of arguments about how it was going. That's one of the reasons it's so weirdly constructed is that everyone was throwing ideas in about it. We never finished it, we just didn't have time to do what we wanted to do with it, really. I don't think anyone was really happy with the finished result. Once again, live it was much better. (TMI)

bill (1994): "Survival" bothers me a bit. It was kind of an early ecology song. That melody sounds a bit drippy to me. "Sweetness" and "Survival," you could junk both of those, I think. (TMI)

TIME AND A WORD
RELEASED AUGUST 1970
(U.S. RELEASE NOVEMBER 1970)

Time and a Word showed a band more confident in the studio and more involved with the actual production of the record. Unfortunately, it still fell short of what the band felt it was capable of creating. The decision to have a string section play a major part in these sessions met with mixed results. Occasionally it would enhance what the band was doing, but more often it would smother or take away from Yes's own arrangements.

This was also the time of the band's first major personnel change. Peter Banks was fired from the band for reasons that are still unclear and his guitar work on this record was put down low in the mix or simply eliminated from the songs. The band chose the multitalented Steve Howe (formerly of Bodast and Tomorrow) as their new guitarist and went on the road to support the record. But *Time and a Word* was destined to sell very few copies.

bill (1970): The difference between the first and second LPs is im-mense. Consequently I envisage a huge improvement between the second and third. (MM)

jon (1982): I had speakers at the bottom of my bed, blasting out classical music all the time. So in one ear there was rock, and in the other ear was the classics. I was interested in opening up the sound of the band, developing a string sound, and we talked about trying a Mellotron, but we thought it only had a certain sound, and that it relates to only a certain type of music. We did try it out a couple of times, then we decided to use real musicians, strings and brass and things like that. So in some ways, it was kind of an adventure, really. For the most part it worked, but sometimes the musicians weren't really up to it. They were session men, but they didn't sound like they were really up. They were just doing their job. (RR)

bill (1994): In the early days huge lumps of music were borrowed from classical music. Sibelius and Stravinsky stuff was stolen lock, stock, and barrel. And we used to steal Vanilla Fudge–style arrangements and the Fifth Dimension was very popular. One of Jon's favorite bands was the Fifth Dimension, which is basically now a cabaret group in the States, I think. A close harmony vocal group. He had an album by them and he wanted vocal harmonies in that style and so the influences were pretty diverse, really. Yes music moves from bits of jazz to bits of Beatles to bits of Shostakovich to bits of the Fifth Dimension. (TMI)

peter (1972): When I heard the final mix of the album, I was very upset. I felt like crying; the guitar was gone. The guitar virtually disappeared. (PR)

(1994): Nobody was more dedicated to the band than I was [at the time]. And to see my contribution minimalized was difficult.

The second album was a big problem because basically the producer—and I use that word very carefully—Tony Colton was a singer; he'd never produced an album before in his life. He was a friend of Jon's and I don't know where Jon met him. But Tony Colton didn't like me personally and he certainly did not like my playing. So the recording of that album was very strange, to put it mildly. The orchestral augmentation was something I didn't want and I think most of the guys didn't want [it either]. Because the whole point of Yes was to make ourselves sound like a small orchestra without any other assistance. This was all very much a thing of Jon's. When we went in to do that album I had a big problem with the orchestral augmentation, because some of my guitar parts were played by strings or brass and the same with Tony Kaye. So consequently we didn't get to play those parts or if they were played they were taken out of the mix. (TMI)

eddie offord, engineer/producer (1995): I'd known Tony [Colton] for a long time up until that point. . . . I liked him a lot, but I don't think he was right for Yes particularly. (TMI)

ON YES COMPOSING CREDITS

bill (1994): I'll always refer to them as band compositions, although of course in those days, normally the guy who wrote the words and sang the top line was the writer for the publishing thing. Of course the arrangements we spent hours on . . . hours in the rehearsal room on the arrangements.

As a young man I didn't understand about publishing credits or publishing royalties. Nobody told us any of this stuff. I had to learn about the music industry while I was in it and I have done my entire life. So I didn't understand the fact that everything that was credited to Anderson was going to make him five times richer than me. I was happy to be tossed my few scraps. That was okay, and I had lots of control over the rhythm and the textures of the songs. I was happy and all of my suggestions were enthusiastically kept within the band's music. (TMI)

peter (1994): I certainly had a hand in writing these songs, but you don't see my name on them at all. At the time it didn't really matter, but of course now it's a whole different thing. I was talking to Patrick Moraz about this same subject when I saw him in New York a couple of months ago. He's had the same problems with his contributions. But at least he's got his name on there; I don't even have my name on. Now it's very much a financial thing, but it's also a matter of respect and being treated on an equal basis. (TMI)

"No Opportunity Necessary, No Experience Needed"

peter (1994): It was probably Jon's idea to do the song. We didn't do it that differently than Richie Havens except we put in the thing from "The Big Country." I don't know whose idea that was. I always loved that tune. I used to like Aaron Copland a lot and it reminded me of a simplified Aaron Copland kind of thing. That western, big wild west kind of feel and it just seemed to fit in there. It worked in a kind of perverse way. It had nothing to do with the song whatsoever. We used to open the set with that quite often. We used to change our opening number every few months, but I think we finally settled on the ultimate opening tune as being that one. It's very fast and furious. If you could get through that you could get through the rest of the numbers. (TMI)

"Then"

peter (1994): I think we all enjoyed playing that. It was band piece that was a lot more powerful live. It had a lot of light and shade. We always had a lot of dynamics. Not many rock bands in those days were using volume. You were either loud or you weren't loud. Remember most bands in those days were playing twelve-bar blues. What we wanted to do was knock an audience cold, when we were loud we were really loud and when we were quiet we were virtually inaudible. And "Then" was one of those pieces where there was a very big dynamic range. We wanted to be different than everyone else and we were very conscious of that. (TMI)

bill (1994): I remember liking the tune "Then." That's quite nice. (TMI)

"Everydays"

peter (1994): I always liked it. It was originally done by Buffalo Springfield and I think it was probably my idea to do that. I was very much into the California bands, the bands out of San Francisco like Buffalo Springfield, Country Joe and the Fish, and all that kind of thing. It was one of the first tunes we learned and why it came out jazzy like that I have no idea. It was in basically ¾ or ⅝; probably Bill was responsible for the feel of that, I would imagine. Most of the cover tunes that we learned came about remarkably easy. We were just throwing out ideas and they would just evolve. We were all into different musics, but we never had a problem playing. We used to have fantastic arguments all the time, but it wasn't unhealthy. Anyone who was a slacker in that band just wouldn't have lasted. (TMI)

"Sweet Dreams"

jon (1970): I like "Sweet Dreams." I'm writing much more now. I've been writing for about two years and I think I've got a long way to go yet. (MM)

peter (1994): We either had songs like "The Prophet" or we had ones where we actually wanted to do a song and try and keep it simple. That was one where we wanted to do not a pop song, but something that wasn't so flashy or contrived. "Sweet Dreams" was more a song than a band arrangement. Once again live we had problems with that. We never really got into a groove on that. I think it might be my fault. I was still into open chords and I could never be described as a remotely funky player in any way. Whereas now it is completely the opposite. (TMI)

trevor rabin (1995): No one wanted to play that song in 1984. I kept pushing for it and they said, "It's not really a well-known Yes song," and I replied, "Who cares? Let's go deep!" I love that song. (TMI)

"THE PROPHET"

jon (1970): I wrote a song called "The Prophet" about a man everybody follows, like people follow Dylan and the Beatles. But he tells them they should find and believe in themselves and be their own prophets and not just follow like sheep. (MM)

bill (1970): "The Prophet" has about five changes of tempo and key changes before the singing comes in. I suppose it is very easy to be too clever. (MM)

peter (1994): We stole from Gustav Holst's "The Planets" for "The Prophet." I forget which movement, I think it was the fourth one. We used to steal a lot from classical things. Jon was very much into classical music and I grew up with it. And we would say, "Why don't we take that Stravinsky thing or whatever?" And "The Prophet" was another band composition, undoubtedly. It was very good live, we used to have fun with that. I think from a composition standpoint that I wrote a third of that easily. (TMI)

tony (1985): I didn't really like the multilayered business. My thoughts at that time were, "If you're going to use an orchestra, use an orchestra." (K)

"CLEAR DAYS"

peter (1994): Jon wanted to do his "Eleanor Rigby" with a string quartet and it happened. I don't think we were even really consulted about playing on it. I didn't particularly like it. (TMI)

"ASTRAL TRAVELLER"

peter (1994): I still like that. It's one of the few ones I can actually listen to and still feel quite comfortable with. That is certainly more my song than anyone else's. That one started off with the guitar riff. A lot of our tunes came out of jamming. We were real rehearsal junkies. We used to rehearse a lot and usually someone would come in early. Bill was usually there first and was banging around and I would pick up my guitar and join in. Our old manager Roy Flynn had a basement under his house that we set up in. So we were very lucky to have a place when we weren't gigging to leave the gear set up. Because if you booked a rehearsal studio the gear had to be moved in and out the same day. A lot of the things would come out of just Bill and I playing. "Astral Traveller" came out of a jam. The guitar riff I thought of and builds up off that. Certainly all of the chords there are mine. (TMI)

"TIME AND A WORD"

peter (1991): We wanted an anthem song. Jon came in with the initial idea and he's not the world's greatest guitar player, he was kind of limited to two or three chords which he'd bang out and they'd all sound the same to me. He sang this song and we tried to figure out what he was trying to play . . . "What are these chords, really?" I don't think any of us liked it at the time and we had trouble playing it live. It was a simple song, done simply. (YHS)

(1994): The thing with Jon is that if he's playing a wrong chord, and often it is, he's one of those people who didn't like to be proved wrong. He'll say, "No it's this chord because I wrote it and that's what the chord is!" And I used to have many arguments with him and I'd say, "No, it's wrong chord. It sounds wrong." And then eventually I would change it and maybe he wouldn't notice or he'd say, "Oh, that's the chord." Like that was what he had in the back of his mind anyway and I was just the instrument that received this divine knowledge. . . . I was upset at the time because a friend of Jon's named David Foster actually played acoustic guitar on it. I didn't like this idea at all. I figured I was the guitar player, why is this guy playing guitar? . . . I just played over the acoustic guitar track, which wasn't even supposed to stay on there. It was just a guide track. I think what I played Tony Colton didn't like at all and it never went down on tape or it went down on tape, but was never used.

I remember the day "Hey Jude" came out we heard it on the radio. It was late at night and we had just done a gig in a London club. And I remember sitting in the car and they played the full version of it. In those days it was quite a big deal because it was a long tune. And Jon was very impressed with it . . . Jon wanted to do something like that. (TMI)

ON PETER LEAVING

If Yes was a building, it would definitely have a revolving door in its lobby. In its twenty-six-year history Yes has never had the same lineup of musicians for more than two albums in a row. The change in personnel was usually the result of musical and personality differences, but it has always helped to push the group into new musical directions. . . .

chris (1994): The motto of this band has always been "You'll See Perpetual Change." (TPRS)

peter (1991): I was kicked out! One of the first of many, I might add. It was kind of brutal how it was handled. I was extremely unhappy about it.

Especially since Bill and I were still sharing an apartment at the time . . . by sharing I mean separate rooms obviously! (WS)

THE YES ALBUM
RELEASED MARCH 1971

The Yes Album was the first classic record the group had created and they were well aware of it. From the opening chords of "Yours Is No Disgrace" to the wonderful guitar passages that close "Perpetual Change," it was the first time they had fulfilled the vision of what Yes should be.

It was an arduous journey to get the record made at all. Atlantic Records was having second thoughts about giving the group the opportunity to make a third album and came very close to giving them the ax. Fortunately that move was reconsidered due to some campaigning by Phil Carson and Neshui Ertegun, people at the label who believed in Yes. To make matters worse, financially things within the band were not well. Everyone in the group was used to starving for his music, but this time was especially bleak. Yet they were able to escape their problems by writing and rehearsing the music for this record intensely on a farm in Devon, England. It is a testament to them as musicians that despite the circumstances around them they were able to create such a fine album. The interjection of Steve Howe took the band onto another level and Yes correspondingly moved directly into the world of Progressive Rock. *The Yes Album* was the band's first major artistic and commercial success and on its strength they were able (as an opening act) to tour America for the first time.

jon (1994): I actually saw Steve a month before we got together, when I went to the Speakeasy and he was playing. I remember walking right past him, underneath the stage, just looking at this guy with this beautiful guitar, playing so many notes and so clear singing away with his guitar. And his name came up a month later and I said if he'll join let's go for it. (ITS)

(1971): We decided to get Steve in when we found out he was mad. You have got to be mad to join us. (MM)

steve (1993): Chris had seen me playing in various groups like Tomorrow and the In Crowd. So Chris called me up and said, "Hey, are you interested in this group? It's real big-time. We've got loads of bucks to buy new equipment and a record deal and everything." And it sounded very rosy. It started off like that for about a week. We'd done a rehearsal together. And I said I liked the idea of it and I did, really. So it sort of led on from there. Then it got tough again. Because only a couple weeks after I joined . . . Yes sort of simulated Bodast and other groups I'd been in by not having two pennies to rub together. (GTRSP)

(1982): I had ideas that would flow and go with their ideas. Peter had ideas too, but with the collective group. When I came in, all of a sudden my ideas were a little off the wall for a guitarist. I liked to play jazzy bits, like in "Perpetual Change," which Peter had been doing also. I'll give Peter his credit: He was utilizing different styles. But I felt, "Aye yeah, I can replace Peter." (R)

Patrick Moraz.

Peter Banks at home, 1995.

bill (1994): Around the time of rehearsals for *The Yes Album* we were down to our last thirty bucks, our last fifteen pounds. We all thought the group had broken up around then. We just managed to keep ourselves alive. It was a very bleak period after the second album where nothing had really happened at all. And we were still stunningly unfamous! Even though everyone said we should be famous. Bands don't get that long now, three years into our career and we were still in staggeringly bad shape. I think the feeling was in those days, you give a band three albums, pretty much. Now you'd have about three seconds, so there's no chance to develop anything at all. So I was grateful to be a young musician at the time I was a young musician. (TMI)

steve (1993): When I made *The Yes Album*, I played it on a mono record player and thought, "This is terrible. This is no better [than] anything else I ever made." But as the years passed I realized that it was one of the first masterpieces I was a part of. (MNN)

eddie (1995): After *Time and a Word*, Yes said we think you're terrific and we really don't feel like we need an outside producer—how about on the next album we produce it all together? *The Yes Album* was the first record I'd had my hands on producing and it was the first hit for Yes, and it was my first hit as a producer. It was great, you know?

We developed a situation where the band would write skeletons of songs in rehearsal and they were just skeletons. When we got into the studio, we would record every song in about a minute or a minute and a half section with just drums, bass, and maybe a scratch guitar. On the twenty-four-track tape there was a splice every minute or so and when you rewound it to the beginning of a song you'd hear the edits go by . . . swish . . . swish. We'd be in a song a little bit and someone would say, "Let's try to put an acoustic section here, let's try this here . . ." It was all very experimental, but we kind of built it up as we went along. When the album was finished, and this applies to all of the next few albums, the band would then have to take the studio tape and go and learn how to play it as a band, because it wasn't worked out that much ahead of time.

(1995): When the band first started developing, Jon especially wanted Yes to be a real vocal band. And back in the early days no one could sing to save their lives, except for Jon! Chris was pretty bad, but Steve was the worst! When we did the vocals on the first few albums, which are all pretty much double-tracked anyway, I had to take one of them at a time and do it line by line—it was the most tedious thing to get an in-tune, half-decent performance. It was really, really hard. . . . The unlikelihood of them blending actually turned out really good, because they do blend! (TMI)

trevor horn (1980): I've been a Yes fan ever since *The Yes Album* (R)

"YOURS IS NO DISGRACE"

jon (1976): It was Vietnam at the time, and kids were going out there that had to fight, and it's not their fault they had to fight. They had to get into it. They had to get on top of it or else they were going to get killed. They had to get on top of the whole situation. And that's what struck me, that it wasn't a disgrace to fight, even though the innermost feelings of man is that it's the most cruel, degrading, abysmal thing to be doing is to kill your fellow man. (YMRS)

(1994): I remember when we rehearsed that song, "Yours Is No Disgrace," it was a group activity and it became an instrumental piece of music, far and above a song. It was maybe two-thirds instrumental and the other third was the song. It really has survived the years very, very well, that song. (ITS)

steve (1981): The walking bass lines of "Yours Is No Disgrace" . . . Chris was going "Yesterday, a bum, bum, bum, morning came, vum, vum." That opened an opportunity for an acoustic guitar. So you see all of a sudden I was in a group where I was playing what I wanted to do. I could alter my style depending on the number we were doing. (R)

(1978): I'm fond of the "Yours Is No Disgrace" solo on the original album, particularly because it was a breakthrough to be able to start working like that, overdubbing guitar parts, mixing parts, constructing a piece of music. I'd been wanting to do it for years, but until I joined Yes I didn't have the facilities. It was a "studioized" solo because it was made up in different sections; I became three guitarists. (GP)

"(The) Clap"

steve (1993): I told an audience the other day that it's still a challenge to play, and it really is. I'd say that, at the moment, it's one of the best guitar pieces I've written. I only change it slightly now—I change the dynamics a little to keep it interesting and fresh. It seems to have guitarists outfoxed; very few know how to play it correctly. I just made it up one night. It was written on the night of August 3, 1969. I remember that because my son Dylan was born the next day. So it has a very strong connection with Dylan. (GW)

(1992): "Clap" on *The Yes Album* really defined what I could do on the guitar. It was very much influenced by Chet Atkins and I think it's the main guitar tour de force that I've written. The title "Clap" was actually a total balls-up—I remember turning to Bill Bruford and he said, "call it Clap," because he thought it makes you want to clap along with it. Then when Jon announced it on the record he called it "The Clap." This changed the context for the rest of my life! Atlantic kept insisting on writing "The Clap"—I went through the roof! I just couldn't get away from the distasteful connotations of the title. Since it's one of my best pieces it's annoyed me a lot that it became known as "The Clap"—it had absolutely no reference to things like that! It was supposed to be about clapping along and enjoying yourself! (GTM)

"Starship Trooper"

jon (1976): There is a messenger within you that is always interreacting with the life-form. There's that point in you within yourself that knows you. We call it "God." And it's this point where you say "Mother life hold firmly onto me/ Spread my knowledge higher than the day/ Release as much as only you can show." Because no matter how much you want to get clearer visions of what you're up to, you're only going to get a certain amount. (YMRS)

steve (1992): "Starship Trooper" incorporated bits from everyone but we had to give three credits because Jon wrote the actual song, Chris wrote the middle bit, and I wrote the instrumental end. That took a bit of clarification between us at the time but it paved the way for us to appreciate each other's contributions. . . .

Those early records were recorded on sixteen-track. We did use some recording surgery while we were making those records, which was quite an innovation for us—if we liked something from somewhere we could fly it around to where it worked the best. If we didn't like one note we might change three bars for that one note, so we were quite meticulous. The stereo panning for the guitar solo happened largely by chance—I had recorded two guitar tracks and when we came to mix it we found the best phrases alternated between these two tracks. So we cut one and pulled the other up and vice versa all the way through the solo. "Starship Trooper" was difficult to record because the finished version wasn't quite how we arranged it in the first place—I don't think we ever played it quite like the record outside the studio. We realized that it was quite good fun to have a song that we radically changed in the studio, either because we had hardly played it or we didn't know what to do with it so we just arranged it there and then, much like "Your Move"—we developed a way of recording which had nothing to do with being on stage. "Starship Trooper" benefited from the same techniques—all the climbing and building business in the Wurm section worked pretty well. (GTM)

tony (1994): If I have to play those three chords again, I think I'll throw up! (WS)

"YOUR MOVE/I'VE SEEN ALL GOOD PEOPLE"

jon (1988): There are so many different ways to look at it. Every time I would think " 'Cause his time is time in time with your time" I was trying to say that I will do anything that is required of me to reach God. And I think that whoever is listening to it should feel the same thing, that they are in tune and in time with God. (CL)

(1994): It was a definite idea to have a developing quiet song and then just break open into a full church organ sort of thing. Grandiose, very big. Let's get the cathedral choir in there, that sort of thing. It was a strong feeling to make it grand and then it can go into nothing. Out of that nothing comes a drum roll and then into this funky "Dum-dum-da-dum," which on record is very light. By then we were getting to the actual production of things. Before we had left it to other people. (ITS)

chris (1995): I always liked the riff in "I've Seen All Good People." (CSV)

"A VENTURE"
"PERPETUAL CHANGE"

jon (1973): We were in Devon rehearsing *The Yes Album*, staying in a beautiful valley. Nature was all around us and it was amazing. I was thinking how we zoom up to the moon when our own environment on this planet is all fouled up. The one thing that sparked me off was the fact that they'd been to the moon a few days earlier, and when they left, they sent something back to blow it up to see how thick it was. At the same time we started having the Pakistani flood disaster. So I was thinking, okay you knock the moon off its axis and you're going to mess up the world. (C)

bill (1994): [about the middle section] We were always looking for a couple of lines to go against each other, a bit of counterpoint. Again that was all very art school–classical–art rock type thing. Counterpoint was unknown in rock, there was no such thing as that. To have two contrapuntal lines like that . . . that was considered all very tricky. But bear in mind nobody wrote music at this point. Until Rick Wakeman came in nobody could read a note of music. So all of this was figured out with painful, tortuously slow work. The kind of thing that a half-assed arranger could knock out for you in ten minutes, but for us it took forever and a day to do. (TMI)

chris (1995): That was a thing that Bill Bruford and I were working on, that particular section, the chorus of "Perpetual Change" is in 7/4. Then the other section is a double-time version of 7/4 and so it was the kind of thing where one was designed to fit with the other, because they were both in 7/4 time. The fact that you could play both riffs at the same time made some kind of musical sense and that is why we developed that section; so that one took over from another. I remember I wrote the music for the chorus and double-time riff and Bill and I developed them. I'm sure he came up with the rhythmic idea for the faster riff. It was a rhythm section trip! (TMI)

FRAGILE
RELEASED JANUARY 1972

Chances are good that right now a radio station somewhere is playing a song from this record. Immediately following its release it attained the legendary FM radio status that bands dream about. After an American tour the decision was made to let Tony Kaye go for personal and professional reasons just before sessions were to start for *Fragile*. The very talented Rick Wakeman (of the Strawbs) took his place as the keyboardist for Yes and the record was made in just a few short weeks. *Fragile* was originally going to be a double album, one LP being studio recordings and the other a live disc featuring the cover songs "America" and "It's Love," but that idea was dropped because of the time needed to put it together. In addition to the four major compositions on this record it was decided that each band member would have the opportunity to showcase his talents on an individual solo track. This album also marked the first of many successful collaborations between Yes and the artist Roger Dean. Their music and his exotic, surreal landscapes became irrevocably associated with each other over the years. The band toured incessantly after *Fragile* came out and for the first time were a major headlining act.

jon (1989): We did an American tour that really energized us incredibly. We wanted to get back in the studio and make another album quickly, because we knew that we were on sort of a roll on many levels. And all of a sudden there was this definite feeling of we've got Steve and he's very multitalented and maybe we should look for a more multitalented keyboard player. That's when Rick Wakeman joined the group. He was the darling of the universities and colleges, he was the man to go see. Rick was very talented and individual in his style. . . . He joined the group and again we were injected with that energy. (ITS)

bill (1991): So Tony got the chop and you could see what was happening, you know. The band just got better musicians all the time, as most groups did in those days. You just kicked out the guy you started with and got a better guy. Terrible, isn't it? Terrible, but true. (MTV)

tony (1991): One of the reasons I left the band originally was because I was such a traditionalist in so many ways. I just wanted to play the organ. When I was a piano player, I started playing the organ because I just loved the Hammond sound. When the Mellotron and the Moog came out, I wanted nothing to do with them. I hated those sounds. But the band was pushing forward very rapidly at that point; there was definitely a disagreement. And Rick was getting that stuff together, so obviously having him come in was the right progression for the music. (K)

ON RICK JOINING THE FIRST TIME

rick (1974): I had been doing a lot of sessions and was lying in bed after having done a three-day stint with about six hours of sleep. And that was typical. I had just arrived home having had no sleep again, and fell into bed. It was one of those things where the minute my head hit the pillow, I fell asleep. It felt so good, and then the phone rang. I couldn't believe it, and Ros picked up the phone. I could hear the conversation, "He's only just come in. He hasn't been back for three days . . . you know he's really tired." I was awake by then and let me tell you I was furious. "Gimme that phone . . . who's that?" I said. And this voice said, "Oh, hello. It's Chris Squire from Yes." It's three in the morning and he said, "How are you?" I said, "You phone me up at three in the morning to ask how I am?" I told him I was very tired and asked him if he would phone back. "Well," he said, "We've just come back from an American tour and we're thinking of having a change in personnel. I saw you doing some sessions down at Advision Studios and all I wanted to know was if you'd be interested in joining the band." And I, like a prick, said "NO!" and slammed the phone down. I was furious. (RS)

(1989): Then I got a message from Brian Lane, who was Yes's manager, he said, "Why don't you at least have a rehearsal? At least give it a try and see how you feel from there." And I said all right. So I went along at this rehearsal the following morning and it was at that actual rehearsal that day that the basis of "Heart of the Sunrise" and "Roundabout" were put together. And it was a strange thing because nothing was really said [about me joining], it was suddenly like seven o'clock in the evening and they said that's the end of rehearsal. And Steve Howe couldn't drive and I said, "Steve, where do you live?" And he said, "Hampstead." I said, "Well, I'll drop you off. Look, I live in Harrow and I literally pass by your door, should I pick you up in the morning for rehearsal?" And he said, "Okay, fine." And it's strange because nothing was ever really said, that's it.

We had a rehearsal together and we ended up writing in the first week "Heart of the Sunrise" and "Roundabout." Which just completely freaked me out. I came back really excited because I felt here was something . . . that if this didn't capture the people's imaginations, then it really was back to the sessions, because I really was too left field or something. (ITS)

jon (1989): I think it took about four or five weeks to record *Fragile*. Rick coming into the group made us work faster and harder than we'd ever done before. We were working sixteen-hour days without stopping really, maybe one day off every couple of weeks. It was an inspired time, totally inspired by the music. The music we were working on was so new and so fresh to us that it was pretty easy to get out. (ITS)

rick (1989): I couldn't believe the attention to detail. I mean we would spend three or four hours just musically discussing three bars—whether the link was right or not. And trying it all sorts of ways and then coming back to the way we started. I thought, "This is totally over the top! This is totally unnecessary." But at the end of the day after all those hours were put into the little bits . . . when you listened back to the tracks you realized that it was those little attentions to detail that make the pieces what they are.

I was always convinced—and it sounds egotistical and I don't mean it to— that when we did *Fragile,* all the time that we were recording it, writing it, and putting it together that it was something very, very special. (ITS)

steve (1987): I think of Yes in '72 and '73 with *Fragile* and *Close to the Edge.* That's when we reached our highest point with the best intentions. I would also say those were the definitive band members. (G)

chris (1972): Our success in America has to do with our ability as a performing band. I think we've sold records because of that, as much as the records were good. (I)

bill (1994): The first idea I got of any success was sitting in a limo, [in] New York perhaps. And somebody was showing me *Billboard* and I think *Fragile* was number four on the American charts and above us was Frank Sinatra and a couple of other people. It said *Fragile* by Yes and all I can remember is what a pathetically short word the word Yes seemed and a vague feeling that somehow we had done it. I think the minute the band became popular my overriding memory was that somehow we'd pulled off a band heist. It felt like somehow we had gotten away with it and really it was much more exciting doing the bank heist than running away with the riches. Somehow getting there is much more interesting than arriving. (TMI)

alan (1994): A lot of the material prior to my joining the band was the groundwork for the foundation of it being successful. Throughout the twenty-two years I've been playing that music I've grown to love it and play it on stage with as much depth and thought as was originally in the music to begin with. I basically like all of those songs, mostly the stuff from *Fragile* that we played and things like that. *Time and a Word* we didn't play so much, we did things like "Sweet Dreams" and we've done "South Side of the Sky" [from *Fragile*] a few times. But most of the material was from *Fragile* and *Close to the Edge*. (TMI)

ON THE USE OF ROGER DEAN

alan (1991): The actual images on the record covers went with the music. I think it was a definite stamp on the band that helped them get through all of those earlier albums. Where someone would buy an album and take it home and say on the telephone to a friend, "Oh, you've got to hear the new Yes album. You should see the cover!" (MTV)

"ROUNDABOUT"

steve (1987): When we recorded "Roundabout" we thought we had made one of the all-time epics. Jon Anderson and I wrote that in Scotland. It was originally a guitar instrumental suite. You see, I sort of write a song without a song. All the ingredients are there—all that's missing is the song. "Roundabout" was a bit like that; there was a structure, a melody and a few lines. When the Americans wanted us to edit it for a single we thought it was sacrilege. Here the song was so well-constructed and quite over the top— but in the end we did have to edit it. The song did very well. In fact Jon and I won an award for it in 1972. (G)

jon (1989): We were traveling from Aberdeen through to Glasgow and we'd started this song . . . me and Steve were singing it in the back of the van on the way down. One of the things you'll drive through is a very winding small road that goes through this incredible valley and the mountains are sheer from both sides of the road—they just climb to the sky. And because it was a cloudy day, we couldn't see the top of the mountains. We could only see the clouds because it was sheer straight up . . . I remember saying, "Oh, the mountains—look! They're coming out of the sky!" So we wrote that down: Mountains come out of the sky and they stand there. And we came to a roundabout right at the bottom of this road and within twenty-four hours we were back in London. We'd been on tour then for about a month. So it was sort of twenty-four hours before I'll be home with my loved one, Jennifer. So the idea was twenty-four before my love and I'll be there with you. In around the lake—just before you get to Glasgow there's a lake— a very famous one—the Loch Ness. So we were driving in around the lake— mountains come out of the sky—they stand there. (ITS)

steve (1982): [The intro is] the easiest thing in the world to play. I could show anybody and they could play it. But because of sound and the intensity, so nice and strong . . . that in itself is a different kind of connection. It's not that the music or musical idea is that good. It's the come-on, the intensity. One of the secret ingredients of Yes wasn't only the sort of material we were using, it was the intensity of the color. Maybe the beginning of "Roundabout" without the backward piano wouldn't have been so dramatic. People don't even know it's a backward piano, all they hear is "mmmmmweeng!" But it really intensified that idea and I think that's a good side to the music that I have been involved in. (R)

eddie (1992): Yes, a backwards piano. It took quite a long time to assemble it, because it meant picking the right notes and editing it all together. (M)

chris (1994): I overdubbed my entire part an octave higher on one of Steve's old Gibson hollow-body jazz guitars. We just miked it acoustically and mixed it in with the bass. That's what gave the part such a bright sound. (BP)

(1985): "Roundabout" was done in a series of edits. That was the time when we started getting into that idea. Although we'd already played the song in rehearsal, we'd go in the studio and get the first two verses really good. (G)

jon (1989): We always tried to make sure we had a lot of harmony. Me, Steve, and Chris singing together had a certain texture and we worked on that all the way through that period of time. And the strong melody [was] sometimes very, very simple. On the end of "Roundabout" we sing "Da-da-da-da-duh-duh-da" a very simple melody repeated eight times. Over that there's another melody "Ba-ba-ba" . . . "Three Blind Mice!" (ITS)

steve (1994): Jon used to say to me, "I come to you, you don't come to me enough." And maybe he was right and that was Jon's strength to come over to my way more than I went to his. I don't think that's a misgiving . . . I was prepared. I would have my guitar and my tapes and we would get together and we could make the time for that. That's why we wrote "Roundabout." It's one of the first things that we did collaborate on. (TMI)

peter (1994): The main riff in "Roundabout" [Em, F#m, G] I certainly wrote. We were messing about with that years before [*Fragile* was released] and when I heard that come out I was a little sick about it. I understand that people keep these things in reserve, but I think the person who wrote it should be credited for it, it's as simple as that. A lot of these riffs were things that we would jam on when we were rehearsing. Often before we would work out a song we would jam. Somebody would start something, I would or Tony would start a riff, and later it would find its way into a song. With "Roundabout," I know that is something I specifically came up with. (TMI)

"CANS AND BRAHMS"

rick (1973): "Cans and Brahms" was dreadful, but contractual hangups prevented me from writing an original solo track. (RWCC)

[Rick originally recorded a piece called "Handle with Care" that was later reworked into "Catherine of Aragon" for his first solo album *The Six Wives Of Henry VIII*.]

"WE HAVE HEAVEN"

jon (1989): We had four major songs and just before we started doing some more I said to the guys, "Hey, listen, I'm going to go downstairs and I'm going to do this idea that I have. I'm not sure what it's going to be, it's just a rolling idea of voices and things." And I said to Rick, "We'll all do little individual ideas as well as the songs that we've got, which are very strong. We'll have five sort of vignettes." And I went downstairs in Advision into the studio two and recorded a song "We Have Heaven." Which is a vocal musical sort of thing. (ITS)

eddie (1995): Jon would say, "I've got this idea—we're going to put some bombs here." And I'd say, "Well, let's give it a shot and mess around with it." We'd listen back to it and Jon would say, "It sounds pretty good, we'll just put in the background with echo and it'll sound great. I've got another idea . . . we'll put it in the background with echo and it will be beautiful." And this would go on for a little bit and then Bill stood up in the control room and said, "Why don't you put the whole fucking record in the background with echo and be done with it!" It was really a classic statement, because Bill was much more of a purist. (TMI)

"SOUTH SIDE OF THE SKY"

jon (1989): I'd read a little article that said sleep is death's little sister. I thought it was poetic in many ways because most of us don't have a real clue as to what death is really about. It's always been used in very dark terms . . . you're going to die! There's a very strange attitude about it. Because life is very beautiful, why shouldn't death be beautiful? And death be the next extension of life? So that was "South Side of the Sky," the attitude that we keep climbing that mountain, we keep pushing harder and harder to reach the top of the mountain. When in order to reach the top we have to go through transitions and part of that is eternal sleep or the next life span. It was very mystical, that "South Side of the Sky." (ITS)

chris (1995): Jon wrote the initial verse, roughly on the acoustic guitar, and I wrote the riff that went with the chorus to fit with Jon's strumming parts. And the whole of the other middle section was something that I had been working on at home. Rick played the piano solo, he and I worked that section out together. I don't know why we didn't do it live too much. I think we tried it and it didn't really come off that well, sometimes songs don't. (TMI)

steve (1994): The riff from that song comes from "Tired Towers" by Bodast [the intro guitar riff]. Basically we just lifted some stuff from that, because to me Bodast was a closed book and that's why "Nether Street" went into *The Yes Album* [on "Starship Trooper"]. I wasn't trying to start a trend with doing that in my career, splitting up music like on *Turbulence* and *Union*, but it's a long ways between! Chris was responsible for the nice riff on the chorus do-de-do-do-do. That's a terrific riff, it's in three-part harmony and it shows how hard we worked, we did that so much. "South Side of the

Sky" was hammered together more in the studio than anywhere else. It was a studioized number. We didn't rock 'n' roll like that in rehearsal rooms. In rehearsal rooms we played in an organized Yes stylistic way. And yet in the studio if we wanted to add something to the song except for the middle section, we'd kind of rock out! . . . We never could play that on stage. We did it a couple of times, but the vocal section came up short. The vocals were hard to do. And also the way it is played it sounds so beautifully studioized and that's the way it is. It wasn't much of a stage section so we just chucked it out and just played it as an encore, because it was just a rock thing and we could just hammer away. (TMI)

"FIVE PERCENT FOR NOTHING"

bill (1995): "Five Percent for Nothing" was my first attempt at composition—of course completely naive, but we've all got to start somewhere. (TMI)

[The title of "Five Percent for Nothing" was originally "Suddenly It's Wednesday." It was changed to make a reference to paying off their old manager Roy Flynn with the promise of five percent of future royalties.]

"LONG DISTANCE RUNAROUND"

jon (1989): To me "Long Distance Runaround" when I think about it was how religion had seemed to confuse me totally. It was such a game that seemed to be played and I was going around in circles looking for the sound of reality, the sound of God. That was my interpretation of that song, that I was always confused. I could never understand the things that religion stood for. And that through the years has always popped its head up in the songs I've been working with. (ITS)

steve (1994): It seems that there was an interesting clarification when Yes began about the way things were credited and in fact it became all right for some of the time. At other times lots of work was done on songs like "Long Distance Runaround," where the first riff was collaborative. It was a bit of mine and Bill was humming stuff and Rick was harmonizing. (TMI)

"THE FISH"

chris (1991): I think I was just naturally trying anything, just enthusiastic to give things a go. I experimented a lot. For "The Fish" I think I used almost all of the sixteen tracks. (CSV)

["The Fish" is Chris Squire's nickname, bestowed upon him for his long sessions in the bathtub. Not so coincidentally, his astrological sign is Pisces.]

"MOOD FOR A DAY"

steve (1992): I used a Condo Flamenco guitar on "Mood for a Day"— it was similar to my Ramirez and I wish I had never sold it because it had a really nice sound. But then again, my taste in guitars had changed. It was obviously written a bit like a Flamenco piece and the guitarist I was listening to at the time was Sabecas—admittedly, he does have a commercial streak in him but he also has a very strong Flamenco side. I also had records by Carlos Montoya and I think I did sort of base the beginning of "Mood for a Day" on a piece by him, but I can't remember what it was called. Of course you always pick up things from listening to records—I don't think there's anything wrong with that. At the time I had settled down and just started new roots in my life and "Mood for a Day" was supposed to represent a happy mood for a day. I was about twenty-eight when I realized there should be something more in my life than just the guitar. (GTM)

"HEART OF THE SUNRISE"

jon (1994): When I work on music I get a strange feeling at a certain point of time. "Heart of the Sunrise" is that feeling that I get, it's a sort of feeling of completeness when we finish a piece of music and it rings true to my chakra energy, my consciousness. (YV)

(1989): "Love comes to you and you follow," it's the spirit of love within and you follow that spirit of love, you dream it, and you make it become a reality. And the heart of the sunrise is an incredible energy, but I tend to think there's a more unifying level, a more spiritual level, a more cosmic level to it, and having actually found and witnessed one or two extra dimensions on this planet, I know for a fact it isn't just a ball of fire. So the heart of the sunrise is something that energizes the within of the beings we are. We are all the same, we are human functional beings with a soul which is all one. (Q)

steve (1992): It was Chris who wrote the main riff. I always thought the riff was influenced by [King Crimson's] "21st Century Schizoid Man," but I suppose we got away with it. It's a really powerful track and like many Yes arrangements it's strangely individual—we start with a big thing, drop down, build up, then there's a song. It's clever how Rick's influence showed a lot on that album with what we called the "Rick-recapitulation" bit where we would go back and play fragments of previous segments interspersed with Rick's piano. (GTM)

rick (1975): One of my all-time favorite songs—not just because I played on it—is "Heart of the Sunrise." Incredible tune. (RS)

(1973): I like Jon's lyrics; they do make you think and derive your own meaning from them. I couldn't understand "Heart of the Sunrise," originally, but I derived my own meaning from it. There's no "I love you baby, come to bed, let's do a 69 and dig my knees," about Yes. (RWCC)

chris (1985): I've always had my favorite tracks. I used to like "Heart of the Sunrise" a lot as a piece of music. I thought that it was the most complete but precise example of what Yes was doing. (G)

(1995): Jon wrote the song. He used to go on acoustic guitar and strum these very perfunctory kind of chords and we'd kind of window-dress it after that. That opening riff was something I had been working on, I think Steve Howe had the second riff, and that's how it all came together. It's still one of my favorites. (TMI)

bill (1994): I can remember little bits of music that I put and riffs and ideas. We were all doing it together, really, and I can't really remember the bits that are mine and the bits that are Chris Squire's and so forth. It took a very long time, of course, and somebody having a vague idea of how it should go, but none of us really did. We were very lucky to get the arrangement that we did get. It's a nice one, isn't it?(TMI)

CLOSE TO THE EDGE
RELEASED SEPTEMBER 1972

This is considered by many to be the definitive Yes album. Everything the band was trying to do was uniquely realized on this recording, so that even now it sounds as fresh as the day it came out. It was a very successful and progressive release at the time, featuring just three songs: the celestial "And You and I," the fiery "Siberian Khatru," and their first masterpiece epic, "Close to the Edge."

The making of this record was not without the loss of some blood in the process. After the laborious rehearsals and endless late nights at Advision Studios, Bill Bruford decided to leave Yes when the album was completed, to join King Crimson. His decision left his band mates in shock and desperate because an American tour was to start within a week. (Bruford did offer to do the tour, but the band decided to try to find someone else.) Luckily for the group, Alan White (of the Plastic Ono Band) agreed to climb up the drum riser and he has been with them ever since.

bill (1989): *Close to the Edge* had a sense of discovery for us—and presumably for the people who bought it. I'm sure it sounds trite now, but in those days it was quite a big deal. Rock musicians hadn't been capable of an arrangement of any kind of complexity at all. But now I find it's fundamentally good music, its form, its shape are timeless. (Q)

jon (1992): I think there was a unified feeling about doing *Close to the Edge* that was a moment in time. It'll never happen again and never will happen again the way that happened. It was the weather, it was London, it was Advision Studios, it was the atmosphere, it was the collective knowledge that we were embarking [on something] a little bit new, a little bit of uncharted territory. And I think that's one of the things that makes *Close to the Edge* as perennial as it is. (ITS)

steve (1993): My first three Yes albums—*The Yes Album, Fragile* and *Close to the Edge*—are all pretty much of the same ilk. They were done in quite a short, very intense span of time, and to me they are pretty inseparable. I like all of them for different reasons, but currently, looking back, I quite like *Close to the Edge*. (GW)

jon (1992): *Close to the Edge* is close to the edge of realization, of self-realization, that's what the theme was all about. It was based on a book I'd read called *Siddhartha* by Hermann Hesse. So there we were on the edge of learning about our potential as artists, as musicians in order to jump into a new world of music. That's what *Close to the Edge* was all about and it did push us in a direct fashion into the limelight, one could say, of total progressive music. To the point where today, we can perform nearly twenty years later "And You and I" and it has more power now than it ever had. It's a remarkable piece of music, as though it was crafted by the heavens and we were just the vehicles to pull it together. (ITS)

bill (1992): If we'd known how horrible it was going to be, we would have never done it. But it's like five guys trying to write a novel at the same time. One guy has a good beginning and the second guy had quite a good middle and the third guy thinks he knows what the ending is, but the fourth guy doesn't like the way the middle goes towards the ending, and the second guy who used to like the third section has changed his mind and now likes the first section.

It was torture. None of these arrangements were written and they weren't really composed. We all sat in the rehearsal room and said, "Let's have the G after the G#." And every instrument was up for democratic election, you know and everyone had to run an election campaign on every issue. And it was horrible, I mean it was incredibly unpleasant and unbelievably hard work. And Squire was always late for every rehearsal. And after about two months of this unbelievable punishment, people still say to me, "Bill, why didn't you do another one?" (ITS)

(1994): Nowadays of course everyone's more professional and everything takes nine months or two years now. But we were running pretty fast as musicians. We were all nineteen years old and very wired. There was a lot of coffee being drunk.

When we set up to record an album, we didn't record an album all the way through beginning to end, necessarily. We would often break equipment down, drive up the motorway, do a concert two hundred miles away, and come back, set the equipment up again, and we'd continue. We sometimes did this in the middle of tracks, so we'd be halfway through some interminable thing like "Siberian Khatru" or "Close to the Edge" or something. And it would come Friday and we'd break the equipment down and destroy the drum sound—such as it was—drive up the motorway, do the concert and come back and continue playing bar seven. It wasn't so sophisticated in those days, you stuck the same mikes in roughly the same place and hoped for the best.

People always imagine that there was this carefully structured plan. Like they do with King Crimson, they always imagine Robert Fripp enters the room and scowls at everybody and lays out sheet music, which of course is the exact opposite. And they always think that Jon Anderson somehow knew how *Close to the Edge* was going to be right from the beginning to the end. [Which is] not true at all . . . it was kind of a shambles from beginning to end, the whole thing. It was a miracle that we managed to make anything of this stuff. If we'd actually find a rehearsal room, could we actually get to it? Would Squire turn up? Would we have enough equipment to do it with? Was anyone starving? Was the band about to run out of money?

We were well served in all of this by having the ability to tape-edit. And having Eddie Offord, who would slash a two-inch master tape without even

thinking about it and just glue another bit onto it. Tape editing was fundamental to this band creating this music at all. Because we couldn't play any
of it through until we'd learned it. We'd play a thirty-second segment and
say, "What happens now?" We'd stop the tape and write another thirty-
second segment. It would go on like that, [like] climbing Mount Everest.
(TMI)

eddie (1995): I had been on tour with the band for a while and I'd
just been in studios before that. Being on the road with Yes taught me so
much, in that most gigs were average, there was a few really bad ones, and
there was a few really magical ones. For the average person at the concert
. . . even the bad gigs they loved. But after the magical ones it was so obvious,
you just come off the stage and everyone would be like spaced out or
something—floating off the stage. So when we went to do the next album,
not just for the sound—which I was trying to make more live—but also for
the vibe of it, I had the road crew build a huge stage in the studio. So it was
like the band was on stage and the drums had the resonance of the wood
and so on. (TMI)

steve (1991): We had to hang on to our ideas and develop and arrange
them and try not to forget them the next day. Because sometimes we would
come in and say, "God, what did we do to this?" Many classic Yes bits of
arranging have gone out the window. We actually forgot them. They were
too intricate, too specialized, or one guy was the key to it and he was the
guy who didn't remember it the next day. So obviously we taped things and
started to have tapes of rehearsals going on all the time. (YY)

jon (1992): During *Close to the Edge* no one from the record company
came to the studio. They had no idea how long we were doing this piece of
music and what did it all mean. (ITS)
   (1990): Record companies were always a bit fearful of putting out music
that was a bit high on the political end. They would rather go for the status
quo LP and make more money. Now the time is coming when the artists can
be true to themselves and the record companies will be able to make money
anyway. (CL)

rick (1992): My recollection of the time [of *Close to the Edge*] was that
of a certain amount of power, because you knew that just the way people
in the record company and management reacted . . . the best way I can de-
scribe it is that if you are a successful comedian, people will laugh at your
jokes, even if they're not funny! And people started to gather around us like
the proverbial bees around the honey pot or flies around a honey pot, whichever you like to call them. You knew you were hot, you knew you had
something, but to be brutally honest, I don't think any of us knew quite
what it was. The thing we had done on *Fragile* was break a lot of rules. We'd
broken a lot of rules, especially with pieces like "Heart of the Sunrise" and
"Roundabout," with having lots of different moods, tempos, time changes,
everything you shouldn't do on a rock record, we did. And the great thing
for us was that America LOVED IT. It was tremendous, you knew you had
something special to offer, it was very strange. But the other great thing as
well was that we as musicians were ahead of the technology, and we were

ahead of the studios and we were ahead of the record companies and management who had no idea really where we were going, but knew, to put it crudely, that it was making them money so let them get on with it. And that was the secret of Yes and we knew it. (ITS)

"CLOSE TO THE EDGE"

chris (1995): I think it was Jon's idea to open the song with the sound effects. He got hold of a bunch of those environmental tapes and I think that's why it appeared there. (TMI)

eddie (1995): Jon might come up with an idea and I would take it to the max. It took about a thousand tracks to make that opening!(TMI)

jon (1976): The lyrical content became a kind of dream sequence in a way. The end verse is a dream that I had a long time ago about passing on from this world to another world, yet feeling so fantastic about it that death never frightened me ever since. I think in the early days when I was very small I used to be frightened of this idea of not being here—where else can there be if there isn't "here"? And it just seemed a matter of course that death being such a beautiful experience for a man physically to go through as being born is. That's what seemed to come out in this song, that it was a very pastoral kind of experience rather than a very frightening and "Oh gosh, I don't want to die" kind of thing. (YMRS)

(1973): There are several lines that relate to the church. Churchgoers are always fighting about who's better and who's richer and who's more hip. So at the end of the middle section there's a majestic church organ. We destroy the church organ through the Moog. This leads to another organ solo rejoicing in the fact that you can turn your back on churches and find it within yourself to be your own church. (RWCC)

steve (1982): Rick's solo on the organ was actually a guitar part which sounded better on the organ—I was getting quite used to the idea of writing music someone else played. (R)

rick (1992): We'd recorded the whole of the last section, which had to be tagged on to what was already in existence, which was basically after the big organ solo and bits and pieces. And the bin for the scrap tapes we didn't want was out in the garbage, all chopped up. And Eddie had taken the piece that he thought was the right piece and put it on . . . and it *was the wrong piece.* The interesting thing was it was the best performance, but there was an incredible sound change, I mean a really phenomenal sound change which was mainly caused by the echo used on the mix. We all listened to it and looked at each other and there was nothing we could do about it, short of going in and starting recording again, but the odds of getting the same sounds that we had to match on, I mean it was an impossibility. So it stayed! The interesting thing is after about four or five listens it sounded perfectly natural and you can hear it. You can hear on the record to this day and it's an unbelievable sound change, but you know, nobody at the record company ever noticed. (ITS)

bill (1994): We were all so tired, I can't tell you how tired we were. This went on forever and I would begin to doze off on this bench at the back of the room at about one or two o'clock in the morning. And Chris Squire would be talking very slowly about how much EQ there should be on his Rickenbacker bass. And I'd wake up three hours later at five o'clock in the morning and he'd still be talking about how much EQ to put on the bass. . . .

There was a cleaning lady who came in, in the morning. And she was very vicious and would throw away everything. She would tidy everything, but it was a disaster because the record was halfway made so there was tape all over the room and they got taped up all over the wall. As I say I woke up one day at four or five o'clock in the morning and everybody was searching in this trash can for the missing section. It's amazing, isn't it?

The thing about "Close to the Edge" is the form, I think. The shape of it is perfect. It's a real little part of history and it just fit on the side of an album perfectly. Again as we were making that I don't think anyone really knew how we were going to finish it. It felt like we were going on and on adding section after section. Lots of music in different meters and things without anybody really knowing what the conclusion to this piece of music would be. I don't think we had any idea of its length and I don't think we said, "Oh! Let's make this the side of an album." The other thing I remember was everybody saying that Simon and Garfunkel had spent three months on "Bridge Over Troubled Water" and that seemed like a record that needed to be smashed. (TMI)

"AND YOU AND I"

jon (1973): "And You and I" could be classed as a hymn. Not in the sense of a church kind of thing. It's about feeling very, very secure in the knowledge there is somebody . . . God, maybe. (RWCC)

(1994): Every time I sing "Political ends as sad remains will die," I know it's going to happen. If you watch the media, the way the media is so right on Clinton's every move, not just Clinton, but every major leader. Every major politician will come under scrutiny. Because CNN is our consciousness . . . the world is full of incredible stuff and CNN is just the rubbish. And we're centering in on that in order to get rid of it. (YV)

rick (1991): *Close to the Edge* was not just one piece, it was a whole scenario of three pieces. And "And You and I" is like a mini-quintet-sonata in a strange way. It has different movements which all go into each other. The object was of having a piece of music that was everything that the Yes critics hated us for and the Yes fans loved us for, which was emotion. (YY)

chris (1995): I pretty much wrote the instrumental sections. The middle Eclipse part and the Apocalypse part at the end, I brought those pieces of music to it. It was again one of those tunes that Jon wrote. We rehearsed it a hell of a lot before we recorded it and that's why it did very well. (TMI)

steve (1995): We had a very simple song, Jon was strumming three chords and singing, "A man conceived a moments . . ." it was lovely. The way it was presented on the record, I'm sure it wasn't the way we originally

Alan White, the ever-enthusiastic Yes drumr

Steve struts his stuff.

played because there was so many things we did to it in the studio. But besides that, the basic approach to the song was taken saying, "Let's do a pulse to it [the chord progression]." All of the obvious things that happen, I got very happily landed with providing nice big jangly strumming, but in the rehearsal room you can talk about those ideas, but you still have to provide something at the time. When it came to the themes, I think that's where Chris particularly wanted to develop the things. People would say things like, "I like all of that, I just don't like the way it ends." Or someone would say, "I think the chords are too ordinary." Or Chris would say, "I want to play it again, because I can't just play these roots." And he'd have to look for it. So all of that was going on in all of the music and that's how we did it. The way the theme in Eclipse modulates and develops did take a lot of time because Chris, Bill, and Rick were working on it together. They were driving into something really big with Chris's bass pedals.

The intro was integral in the song because it came a second time, so we already knew what we were doing when we did it. I do remember recording that because there is a picture of me sitting in this room that we used to put wooden boards in, it was like a booth, so it wouldn't be so dead [sounding]. That's where we recorded it. . . . There was quite a lot of atmosphere. We were doing something that we were intensely involved in. It was like we were painting this picture together. (TMI)

(1992): I remember the chaos we were in with "And You and I." We had this song, before we knew what happened we had this "Da-duh-duh-da-do-da-do-da-do-da," you know three of those, it was like going somewhere, and we were all going, "But where?" I remember we had "Amen [the IV to I chord progression]," we had these two chords at the end. The first chord was going to go for an indefinite, Vanilla Fudge sort of length, where you were going to hold this chord and everyone was going to boogie on one chord, man! Groove on a chord, you know! It got to be "RRRRRRGGGGGGGGGGGGG," people were playing this note, keyboards were hammering this note, and Bill, I suppose, was hitting something and then eventually with great relief it went "DAAAADUHHHH." And we listened to this a few times and went, "That's a great ending . . . That's a good ending . . . It's not a bad ending . . . It's a average ending . . . It's a pretty lousy ending." Its popularity diminished, you know. Jon and I went out there with voice and guitar and did sort of shape for an ending. We didn't have an end. So in a way we were almost the blind leading the blind. . . . We didn't know what we were doing and this was the marvelous expedition we were on. (ITS)

"SIBERIAN KHATRU"

jon (1973): "Khatru" is just a lot of interesting words, though it does relate to the dreams of clear summer days. The title means winter, but it is meant to be the opposite. It doesn't mean a great deal, but it's a nice tune, and that carries it. (RWCC)

steve (1993): I liked the way "Siberian Khatru" developed on stage and became a real big track to open the shows with—lots of guitar breaks and all that. That song came together with the arranging skills of the band:

Jon had the rough idea of the song, and Chris, Bill, Rick, and me would collaborate on getting the riffs together—it was very much a collaborative thing. (GW)

alan (1995): "Siberian Khatru" was the first song I played with the band, before they recorded it. I was down in the studio and Bill left, they weren't getting on or something. And they said, "Do you want to play on this? It's a bar of eight and a bar of seven." I said yeah! (TMI)

eddie (1995): There weren't the toys that engineers and producers have today, so we had to be really creative and try and find new things. I remember particularly one sound on "Siberian Khatru" on Steve's guitar solo, I had a mike on his amp and I had my assistant take another mike out in the studio with about a twenty-foot cord and swing it around the room so it would have this doppler effect. Those were the kinds of things we used to try! (TMI)

ON BILL LEAVING

bill (1978): There was very much a feeling that we'd cracked it and become famous. Later all that became self-congratulatory, which I didn't really like. I also thought I had done my best with the group and that I couldn't turn in any better ideas than *Close to the Edge*. So then I knew I needed a breath of fresh air. (TP)

(1991): I wanted to be in King Crimson all along. I quite liked Yes, but from where I sat, Crimson looked like a much more interesting band to be in. In fact, both bands were quite interesting and both had their problems. But as a young player, I had, by 1972, been with Yes for about four and a half years, and as a young player, it seemed like a very long time. It seemed like I had been in Yes forever. (YY)

chris (1995): Bill always wanted to let go into the jazz freedom element idea. He didn't like everything to be nailed down too much and then he goes to join a band that makes an album named *Discipline,* so I don't know! (TMI)

YESSONGS
RELEASED MAY 1973

Yessongs is a wonderful souvenir from the Close to the Edge and Fragile tours. It quite clearly captures the band's ferocious energy on stage and is an exhilarating listening experience. Unfortunately, because Eddie Offord was involved in the live mixing of the band, the sound quality of the record is not as good as it could have been. But the stunning performances by Yes more than make up for those deficiencies.

alan (1991): At the time I had just completed a tour with Joe Cocker. I was in Rome when Tony Dimitriades called me and said, "Yes wants you to join the band." As it happened, I was finishing the tour that night, so I flew back to England and we had a meeting in Eddie Offord's apartment. I was sharing an apartment with Eddie then. We had met numerous times through Eddie. Chris had seen me play with Joe Cocker at the Rainbow Theatre in London. Chris and Jon came up to Eddie's apartment and said "Listen. YOU'RE JOINING THE BAND OR WE'LL THROW YOU OUT THIS THIRD-STORY WINDOW!"

(1989): I worked fifty percent of Bill's material to ways in which I prefer to play it and the remaining fifty percent is unchanged due to the framework of the music. Bill was much more of a top kit player, and I had a reputation of being a weighty player. But I think Yes wanted to get slightly heavier within the new music they were creating. (WS)

(1994): It took time for the band to warm up to me and for me to warm up to the band. It's not easy to step in and play such complex material without missing something and those things only come after [playing] awhile. (TMI)

eddie (1995): When Alan first joined the band it took him maybe two tours to even get close to where he should have been at on some of the older material that Bill had played. The first couple of tours Alan was pretty bad, you know? It was hard for him to get all of the licks and stuff. He was really just a great rock drummer. One of the reasons I pushed him on Yes was I always felt that was what Yes needed in some ways, a little more rock to it. As much as I liked Bill I thought it was a little bit too light or something with him. (TMI)

chris (1976): I often felt, even before Alan arrived, that I was possibly playing too much, though I was never really sure. With Bill, the things that I did felt right. But during the transitional period with playing less, just because of his style, I was more careful about what I was doing as well. We had to feel each other out, which is always the case when you change a member of the rhythm section. The drummer and bass player have to hit on a level of what works best for each of them. With Alan, I found that I was able to play a bit less than before and still get my playing across. (BRG)

jon (1973): *Yessongs* signifies an end of an era for us. For the past few years we've been on a continuous cycle of hard work where we tour, record a new album, tour to promote it, then record another album . . . it can go on and on if you let it. Yes has outgrown that now. (RS)

eddie (1995): After *Fragile* I went on tour with the band. At that time I was working with both Emerson, Lake and Palmer and Yes and there was kind of a tug of war going on between the two bands. Because they were both in the same genre. But Yes really wanted me to become more and more involved all the time, so when we finished *Fragile* they said would I consider coming on the road with them. It was really a new thing for a producer/engineer to consider, it was a strange thing for the time. (TMI)

trevor horn (1980): I'll never forget one Christmas I bought my brother *Yessongs* for his present. And on Christmas day we both sat down and listened to *Yessongs* from one end to the other. I had never heard Yes live at the time and I was really knocked out at how good it was. I was fascinated at how Jon had changed the vocal live. . . . "He doesn't do that on 'Starship Trooper,' he goes down on the note in the second line. . . ." That was how into Yes we were. (R)

ON THE MOVIE *YESSONGS*

steve (1981): If you watch *Yessongs* [the movie] you see Yes as I think we should always be. We were working together without conflict—without unnecessary conflict. Somehow, the rate of success, the feeling of success—not all of us were stable enough just to go on and to pretend we were still the same people. (R)

chris (1976): *Yessongs* was one of those films that was made very quickly and organized a day before we did a show in London at the Rainbow Theater about four and a half years ago. And anyone who has seen it will have noted that it's quite dark—you don't see very much. But on the other hand it's a kind of piece-of-history type of film at the time when Rick Wakeman was playing with us. And as a piece of footage it is interesting. It's good history, but it's not a particularly good film. (I)

"OPENING (EXCERPT FROM THE FIREBIRD SUITE)"
"SIBERIAN KHATRU"

steve (1994): We'd used to sing, "Sing, bird of prey, beauty begins at the foot of you," every night before we went on. And you had to be the dressing room five minutes before to do that. It was one of the things we did [to prepare for a gig]. (TMI)

"HEART OF THE SUNRISE"
"PERPETUAL CHANGE"
"AND YOU AND I"

steve (1976): [Sometimes] Yes will perform a song that's rather like the records because we feel we've come up with a good arrangement for it. We can play "And You and I" right down to a line, exactly like it is on record. But I like to do an improvised solo in it. I think it adds something to the way we originally did it. (BRG)

"MOOD FOR A DAY"
"(EXCERPTS FROM) THE SIX WIVES OF HENRY THE VIII"
"ROUNDABOUT"

chris (1994): I don't know if we could ever really do a show without doing "Roundabout," I mean even though as much as I'd like to not do it! (NFTE)

"I'VE SEEN ALL GOOD PEOPLE"
"LONG DISTANCE RUNAROUND"
"THE FISH"

chris (1976): You can play a solo like I did on *Yessongs* that's very trebly and fast, but at the end of the day you always try to put aside what you did, appreciate it for what it was, and try to improve on it. That often means making your ideas a bit simpler—more concise. It's the only way you can keep getting better and I think I am. (BRG)

"CLOSE TO THE EDGE"

jon (1974): When we laid "Close to the Edge" on the audience, we didn't worry about whether they were going to get the full meaning. Music conjures up different ideas to different people, and I don't really feel that it's necessary that everybody interpret what we do in the same way. We're trying to be pictorial—like Dvorak and Stravinsky, if you will. (MHF)

steve (1992): During the Close to the Edge tour I met a doctor backstage. And he said, "This 'Close to the Edge' thing really is quite fascinating in what it's done for some of my patients." We had never really thought about it really, our possible effect on people besides enjoyment in music. We certainly hadn't intended anything like that in the music. But it did make me think, this is an endless quest, to find all the meanings and feelings about music. (MT)

"YOURS IS NO DISGRACE"
"STARSHIP TROOPER"

chris (1995): We had tried to play "Starship Trooper" a few times and it never, ever worked live [at the time]. Not until years later did it start to click. At the time we put it on *The Yes Album* we never played it live, it wasn't until the Close to the Edge tour that it started to happen. Maybe it was because Alan White was in the band that it became a more feasible thing to play live. (TMI)

TALES FROM TOPOGRAPHIC OCEANS
RELEASED JANUARY 1974

This has been a controversial album and will probably always be so. People either love it or hate it, but there is not much middle ground. It certainly was the cause of much friction between the band members themselves, and Rick Wakeman in particular was very unsatisfied with it. *Tales* was a massive undertaking for Yes at the time and a truly demanding and esoteric listening experience for their audience. This was especially true when the band went on tour and decided to play all four sides of the album in their show. Some nights were incredible, but more often the band found that the crowd was unwilling to sit through so much new music. The group adjusted their set accordingly, but after the Topographic tour was finished, Rick Wakeman decided that he'd had enough and left the band.

jon (1974): We've been developing over the years to do eighty minutes of music complete. If you look back to two years ago you'll see that we were then doing twenty minutes complete. . . .

I felt I had to learn from him [Jamie Muir, percussionist for King Crimson]. We started talking about meditation in music—not the guru-type but some really heavy stuff, and he gave me these books of Shastric scriptures. As I read them I became engrossed with the idea of making music around the concepts they spoke of, making a four-part epic built around the four-part themes of which I was reading. (MHF)

(1994): It was part and parcel of an understanding that I was going through, a metamorphosis as a person, and that musically I was growing up and had to flex my muscles and utilize a lot of ideas that were flying around me at the time. And one of them was Yogananda. It was a great learning for me and still is every day. Yogananda was a great man and I wanted to reflect a little bit of that positive attitude towards music into the music for the album. . . .

I spent a year of my life just going crazy, creating a piece of music that even I didn't know what it was all about. I was just driven like a lunatic. Obviously the guys in the band thought that I'd lost it and hated me; it didn't matter. I knew it was this thing I had to do . . . *Topographic Oceans*. If I die after this I'll be happy! (YV)

steve (1992): We had so much space on that album that we were able to explore things which I think was tremendously good for us. Side one was the most commercial or easy-listening side of *Topographic Oceans*, side two was a much lighter, folky side of Yes, side three was electronic mayhem turning into acoustic simplicity, and side four was us trying to drive the whole thing home on a biggie. So we saw them much smaller than they are in reality. Big arrangements, certainly, but we didn't see any problems with it! The critics did, though—it was the most critically knocked album we ever did. We were trying to paint a very big landscape, and when I hear the beginning of side three I can't believe we were going so far out. (GTM)

steve (1981): We rehearsed it in Manticore and I remember sitting on that stage going through some very long arrangements . . . but nobody in the group ever said, "Look, let's bottle out and make a single album." (R)

chris (1987): It wasn't a particularly happy album. It was a busy time then; we were going all the time. It was a major project and there really wasn't enough time to do something that difficult and still capture people's interest as a commercial thing. So it fell a little short. (GW)

(1992): It took a lot of Band-Aids and careful surgery in the harmony and embellishment department to make it into something. At that time, Jon had this visionary idea that you could just walk into a studio, and if the vibes were right, that the music would be great at the end of the day—whether you knew what it was or not. Which is one way of looking at things! It isn't reality. As we know, things need to be looked at more closely to see if they're worthwhile. That's a difficult album for me. (YM)

(1995): Repetition is an important part of rock or pop music. It is the restating of the theme, I suppose, in classical terms. You can't give people too much new material. We have made this mistake in the past as with *Topographic Oceans,* making things too varied and too scattered. People tend to like things that have an attention span focus on it. I wouldn't say short attention span, but some kind of focus on it. (TMI)

rick (1974): We had enough material for one album but we felt we had to do the double. Yes was heading towards avant-garde jazz rock and I had nothing to offer there. (K)

(1981): *Tales from Topographic Oceans* is like a woman's padded bra. The cover looks good, the outside looks good; it's got all the right ingredients, but when you peel off the padding there's not a lot there. I think it's a dreadfully padded album. (R)

When you do albums like *Topographic Go Cart,* it's horrible. Jon Anderson and I are the greatest of friends, and he likes a lot of that album, while I think it sucks. It could have been a sensational album if more thought went into it and if certain parts were thrown out . . . There are some nice parts, but it's like wading through a cesspool to get to a water lily. (MR)

eddie (1995): That album was really a horrific album. Yes albums were starting to take longer and longer as time went by and as there was more money to play with. And since it was a double album it took twice as long to make, maybe even more. At that point it was obvious that Rick became really much more outside the rest of the band. It wasn't so much musical direction. . . . If you want the honest truth it was the fact that the whole band was into smoking dope and hash and Rick was into drinking beer. He never touched pot. I don't know what it was, but he was on the outside. That album almost killed me . . . there was a lot of fighting, even between Jon and Chris. . . .

I think there was a psychological effect of, "Oh, we're doing a double album. Now we can make things twice as long, twice as boring, and twice as drawn out!" . . .

I was really pushing Brian Lane to record the album in a country setting. I thought some flowers and trees would help people chill out a little bit. Maybe it won't be quite so confined as when you're in a town studio. I thought it might give some kind of rebirth, but I argued with Brian for ages about that and the compromise we finally ended up with was we walked into Morgan Studios and there was these large wooden cows and the whole place was filled with trees and plants, trying to appease me somewhat. About halfway through the album the cows were covered in graffiti and all the plants had died. That just kind of sums up that whole album. (TMI)

alan (1994): It was very adventurous thing to do. We wrote the music all together in a place called Manticore in London. It had the sense of a lot of people contributing, but the whole concept was put together by Steve and Jon. Rick was absolutely nuts at the time! We decorated the studio with cows and palm trees. I remember pieces of music that were on bits of tape that were cut out and thrown in the trash can and when we found them we had to stick them back in. Jon decided that one of the songs sounded better when he sang it in his bathroom at home, so they built a bathroom in the studio so he could sing in it. It got quite funny actually. (TMI)

eddie (1995): Today Jon is a really confident singer. He's got an incredible voice and he can hit notes and he's got good control of his voice. But in the early days the vocals were the last thing to be done and the band kept layering and finishing . . . this majestic piece of music kind of arose. As it got time for Jon to put his vocal on this masterpiece, he'd be shaking in the back of the control room. He'd be quaking.

Jon came in one day and said, "It's funny, but when I'm at home and having a bath it sounds so good when I'm singing. I wish it was like that when I was in the studio. Is there any chance that you could do the vocals in my bathroom at home? I know, let's build a bathtub in the studio!" He got some of the road crew and they built a bathtub right in the middle of the studio, but it didn't help at all, of course. (TMI)

alan (1994): There's some pieces of *Topographic* that I knew I wrote pretty much the chord sequences that were kind of longish and I didn't get credit for it, but I'm not going to be picky about that because it was basically Jon and Steve's conception. I was responsible for quite a few of the musical passages in between the main sections of songs. I was kind of mad about it at the time, but it's in the wash, as it were.

In those days we had an arrangement fee, so we'd take ten percent of the publishing and that was the arrangement fee that we all agreed upon. It was everyone's contribution that would make the song work that way. Because the music was so complex everyone would contribute those kind of things, which was the sensible thing to do. (TMI)

chris (1995): It was pretty tough [to perform *Tales* live]. It was quite a tough show to get across to an audience. (TMI)

alan (1995): Everybody thought we were absolutely nuts [to perform all of *Tales* and *Close to the Edge* live]. "You can't do that!" Who says we can't do it? And you know what, not one person left. They were glued there for every concert. It drew you into the music and took you through a journey. (TMI)

jon (1990): One of the dreams that I've had is to really look into *Topographic Oceans* and reissue it on CD as an hour of music, with remixes or overdubs. It could be one powerful idea, but at the time it got bogged down in personality problems—one of the things in attempting a large-scale piece can cause. I've always thought that three quarters of [*Tales*] was an excellent album, with another quarter not quite jelling. In the classic times, an artist would have had time to revise it, but with issue dates the album was out before we really had time to listen to it properly, because you'd have to go out world touring. It was a great effort. There might be a time when it could be performed again. (YM)

"THE REVEALING SCIENCE OF GOD"

jon (1974): It deals with the dawn of light, power, and love. I've had to deal with it on a broad basis, however, because I don't honestly feel that I know everything there is to know about the subject. (BTM)

(1994): It's always delicate to start talking about religious things. Especially when *Topographic* came out, "The Revealing Science of God" should have just been "The Revealing." But I got sort of hip and said, "The Revealing Science of God." A dangerous statement! (YV)

(1993): If you look back there's the old rap song that I used to sing: "Dawn of light lying between the silence of soul sources, chased amid fusions of wonder . . ." [But] it didn't have a backbeat, man! (YM)

steve (1992): People usually laugh when they hear that Jon and I saw side one of *Tales* as being a pop song. That song has got all those intros and then "What happened to this song we knew so well?" To us, this was an accessible song like "Roundabout." We had written it about things that had happened to us, but we thought it translated quite well universally. Originally, side one was twenty-eight minutes long, but we cut six minutes from it—it was still too long for a pop song, though! (GTM)

(1976): I was thinking that I wanted to make it clear, especially on the first side, that if one was going to play in a certain commercial style, then here it was. It was like the whole thing about Zappa doing long solos because the audience wanted it. I was thinking at one stage, "I'll do that. They'll love it." I was playing on the 175 [Gibson guitar], and it came in three main bits. I did the first one, which was a kind of bursting-out style, really high up on the neck so the strings were jumping around a lot. Then I stopped because I couldn't play anymore. I came in, listened to it, decided to keep it, and then went out and played something else. It was right off the top of my head. But because I had that breathing space to stop and think about it, I did the second section like a completely different song. The third section was different again. When we put the whole thing together, it wasn't just a guitar solo. It became, to me, a piece of music. (BRG)

"THE REMEMBERING"

jon (1974): We try to recall our own lives and in so doing get the listener to recall his. It's best described as a calm sea of music and the whole band got involved in playing like the sea—rhythms, eddies, swells, and undercurrents—while we were doing it. (BTM)

chris (1976): One of the nicest things I think I've ever played is on side two of *Topographic Oceans*, "The Remembering." It's a very quiet song, and the bass playing is really gentle. I was playing a Guild fretless and though it's not a hard sound or amazingly fast, I'm prouder of that than I am about some of the things I've played that people rave about. That section starts with a very interesting chord sequence. The key shifts for every bar, and the bass line just happens to bind it all together somehow by following a weird kind of scale. It's a very successful piece of arranging, and when I hear it, I definitely feel that I couldn't have played anything righter, and one doesn't often get that feeling. (BRG)

alan (1974): I wrote the section in part two where Rick plays by himself with the Moog and strings and I wrote a couple more pieces here and there which I put into the whole thing.

(1994): There's a whole section on side two that I wrote the chords to. And I wrote them on guitar and I don't even play guitar! I was playing on the guitar and Jon said, "Keep playing that." And they based this whole section around it. (TMI)

"THE ANCIENT"

jon (1974): It's all about the ancients: civilizations like the Incas, the Mayas, and Atlantis. This one is more of an instrumental track but there is a song at the end which hopefully says that however beautiful a civilization may have been, it has always been wiped out by a power that claimed it was an instrument of God. We tried to interpret the feeling of ancient music throughout the piece and there are times when it really works. (BTM)

steve (1994): Side three is about these mad rhythmic things. There were all of these cues, people going, "When I reach the point . . . Duh-do," everyone would stop on the very next bar. And everyone would have to stop and I would try to do it in about the same place every night, but it couldn't be always in the same place [because of the improvised guitar solo]. There were very tricky little bits, that sometimes on stage would have to get modified, just slightly. Nobody could really agree on the cue so we'd do something else. But imagine the confusion if you get three beats off on a number, a gap in the music! (TMI)

alan (1994): I enjoyed playing side three a lot. I like the whole ethnic kind of feel of side three. (TMI)

chris (1995): The more obscure parts of *Topographic* like side three . . . I don't know whether people should be made to sit through that or not! For a true aficionado of Yes I suppose it would be okay, but I think it's too much for most people. (TMI)

"RITUAL"

jon (1974): At the end of *Topographic Oceans* we put a love song, something very personal. Whenever we sing it, we hope people who listen will understand the possibilities of love. I think many people ask for love, strength, a kind of caressing energy. I remember once feeling very lost and I heard the Beatles sing "All You Need Is Love." I thought to myself, that's it! It gave me such strong rejuvenation. (MM)

It's different in that each member of the band plays a percussion instrument of some sort. There are no vocals or guitars, we all just act like one big drum, which is symbolic of the unity we feel between us. We feel that unity when we play normally, but for us all to do it on one instrument strengthens the whole feeling. (BTM)

alan (1994): "Ritual" is a good piece of music that came to a climax with drums, which was exciting. I did a lot of work on the percussion section and came up with a lot of things like playing the melody with just drums. I was flattered that the band used that as the climax to the whole piece. (TMI)

steve (1994): Some of my favorite playing is my opening to side four after Chris does the introduction, and then I come in with that theme—on stage that was spine-chilling . . . it was heavenly to play.
    I wrote "Life is like a fight," that bit was very close to my on-the-knuckle sort of song about the difficulties [of life]. (TMI)

alan (1995): I played some groundwork piano on the end of "Ritual." Rick wasn't available at the time and so I put it down [the "Hold me, my love" section]. It was something that I wrote and Rick just embellished it later. (TMI)
    We spent a week mixing side four of *Topographic*. We got to the end of the week and felt great that it was finally done and then Eddie Offord was not thinking straight one night and took a razor blade and cut through the master mix quarter-inch tape. It all fell on the floor in pieces and everyone went, "He did WHAT?" He took all the tape home that weekend and put it all back together on his little machine. Can you imagine how many edits there were? (TMI)

ON RICK LEAVING (THE FIRST TIME)

rick (1976): I had some great times and some lousy times. It was a band that was bonded together by music. There was little love lost. It wasn't bad until things got to a stage where I didn't know what direction the music was going in. I didn't enjoy *Tales from Topographic Oceans,* so I finished out the European tour we were doing and left. (K)
    (1988): I've got many failings, but I do have high musical ethics, and I said straight out that I didn't want to play that music and that I thought I should leave the band. This was not to take away from the other guys in the band that felt just as strongly, in the opposite way. It was a very bizarre situation, I was due to start rehearsing with Yes for an American tour, when I decided to call management and tell them I was going to leave the band. Not more than a minute later, A&M Records in London called to tell me that my solo album, *Journey to the Centre of the Earth,* had just gone number one in the charts. On top of it all it was my birthday! It was a strange mixed day. I wasn't happy about leaving Yes, but ethically I had to. (KW)

RELAYER
RELEASED NOVEMBER 1974

Almost immediately after Rick Wakeman had left Yes, the band began rehearsals for this record. As they worked on songs they auditioned keyboardists from around the world, starting with Jon Anderson's friend Vangelis. Unfortunately, Wakeman was not an easy person to replace and the band went through many frustrating tryouts before they agreed on Patrick Moraz (of Refugee). The music on *Relayer* is some of the wildest and most avant-garde the band has ever created, from the war and peace epic ''Gates of Delirium'' to frenzied jazz-fusion of ''Sound Chaser.'' Only on the wonderfully majestic ''To Be Over'' did Yes ease up the hyperkinetic energy. The band went on to a series of extremely successful tours, playing at one gig alone at Philadelphia's RFK stadium to over one hundred thousand people.

patrick (1991): I was invited to have a little jam with the band. I knew what it was all about. They had been looking for a keyboard player for several weeks. They had even tried Vangelis for two weeks, but although Vangelis is a very original player, he couldn't bend to the musical and psychological discipline of being in the band. At that time, I felt it was time to leave Refugee anyway, so I said okay. (K)

steve (1994): Patrick was more akin to what we were talking about. He was a tremendous improviser and dynamic and we wanted the group to be that dynamic. It did have an effect on us all.

We recorded *Relayer* in Chris's garage, which had been converted into a studio. It was almost like Yes had said, ''Okay, we've made this album at this studio, this album at this studio, and now we're going to go to one of the band's studios.'' We put Eddie's stuff in, because Chris hadn't got all his gear yet. I suppose it was one of the first records I ever made that felt like a location record, because all of the others had been made in London. I was looking out the window thinking, ''This is a different way of recording!'' There's nobody telling us the studio is about to close and it didn't cost anything, we could take our time and get things done. It was hard work, but we conjured up some good music.

The studio was semi-makeshift and it was homespun. But we didn't come up with a homespun record, it wasn't Yes gone folky. It was actually Yes with Patrick, which was a very modern, European style of music, and Patrick brought in a South American flavor as well. It was a very international record.

We used to think about making the RECORD. There was a very real fear that all this tape was very well, but how would it go on the record? What would Eddie have to do? He was like a magician as well, he sometimes sprinkled some fairy dust at the cutting of the record! (TMI)

eddie (1995): At that point I'd built my own studio and it was kind of special for them. I used to take this studio on the road with the band and I used to mix sound on it. I just set up at Chris's house and we did an album there on it. It was nice in a lot of ways to have our own place, I think that was really cool. (TMI)

jon (1994): In those days we were making music and we would stop when it was finished and look at each other and say, ''That's great, what is it?'' And they'd say that's twelve minutes long. ''Wow. We'll just tighten that up a bit . . .'' and it's ten minutes long. We were more surprised than anyone that it was long; we just made music until it was finished. (ITS)

Yes takes a break from recording *Relayer* in 1974.
PHOTO BY BARRIE WENTZELL/REPFOTO

chris (1976): I think what Alan and I played on *Relayer* was more to the point. Some of the bass and drum interaction on there is better than anything to be found on previous Yes LPs. But then, it's generally down to the quality of the mixing. With *Close to the Edge, Topographic Oceans,* and *Relayer,* we got into doing many more overdubs, and the more you try to put into that "sandwich," the further back everything gets pushed. (BRG)

patrick (1995): Chris and Jon were always at the opposite extremes. It was necessary to the band that their forces be balanced.

I wish Eddie Offord had been a little less stoned and would have taken his job at the helm of production really seriously, like he did with other recordings. I understand the recording of *Relayer* itself, probably because it was done at a private studio—which was state-of-the-art, though—wasn't as good as some of his other recordings with ELP or previous Yes like *Fragile,* which was extremely well focused and crisp. I think the production of *Relayer* is pretty loose, but the *energy* is there. (TMI)

"THE GATES OF DELIRIUM"

jon (1976): It's a war song, a battle scene, but it's not to explain war or denounce it, really. It's an emotional description with the slight feeling at the end of "Do we have to go through this forever?" There's a prelude, a charge, a victory tune, and peace at the end, with hope for the future.

(1977): "The Gates of Delirium" did not work so well on record, but I think it was a very exciting thing for people to see. The problem was, for FM stations it became more and more difficult to play our music. So all we've had to rely upon is Yes's charisma as a band. Luckily, the fans who come to see us don't come to see a band that's doing well. They have remained loyal to us. (C)

chris (1976): Quite often we won't be working from a song, as such, we'll be working from the music and we get a long way with that. And then, as on *Relayer,* Jon went and wrote the words, even though the tunes and fragments were there, the actual words were written to interpret the music on "Gates of Delirium." (I)

alan (1995): "Gates" was a band composition. I did most of the music for the battle section. (TMI)

patrick (1995): [on the use of sound effects in the piece] I brought this idea with the discussions of concrete music I had with Jon at his house. It just came and grew from that. Once an idea is exposed on the table, you make it grow. I explained to them that on my *Refugee* album I had worked on all the sounds, which accompany the music . . . especially in "Papillon" and "Credo." Also I had explained my experience with soundtracks and sound effects. Jon had also expressed his knowledge of Stockhausen and other music concrete composers at that time. (TMI)

steve (1994): There were some very difficult moments on "The Gates of Delirium," where Jon was getting really excited and carried away with the battle . . . and how we were going to get the battle this way and that way and then we finished it and wanted to doctor it a bit. We were worrying about whether it was a bit too far gone or a bit too safe. One mix was safe and another was too far gone, it wasn't like there was any middle ground to get the battle. We pondered it there for a bit. (TMI)

trevor horn (1980): [on seeing "Gates" live] I can remember when it got to the end and Jon sang "Soon" . . . I felt like crying. It got me so much. I loved that song so much. (R)

"SOUND CHASER"

patrick (1991): [at Patrick's first rehearsal with Yes] We introduced each other, had some tea, and then they played what was to become "Sound Chaser" on *Relayer*—just the middle part, because I would write the introduction later. I was totally overwhelmed, because they played so fast and so precisely and so well. The swing was there. I had never heard such original music, except for what Mahavishnu Orchestra was doing at the time. I must say that I had to have a lot of guts to sit at the keyboards and try to play along. (K)

(1995): Before Steve explained the song to me they played it a couple of times and they were going back and forth to rehearse and to oil some parts. I was just an observer and for me it was a sonic experience that was one of the true sonic experiences of my life. To see Yes at their most powerful and they clearly wanted to impress as well. They will probably say, "Oh, no! We didn't!" But there was this clear feeling that there were the four guys who were trying to impress the guy who was probably going to be the fifth guy. I know exactly how it is, because I've done it with players in my band!

Steve's explanation of "Sound Chaser" was very kind of abstract to me because my English was more succinct than it was three years later. When he said, "Why don't you do five bars of this and move up a tone and go this and digged-duh-la-da and seventeen bars of five and a half . . ." I said, "Let me write down a couple of things!" Some of the notes I played which ended up on the *Relayer* album were from that session. Jon asked me to come up with something there and then and I did that afternoon. I played it and explained it; I wanted to have another part, which actually became the first line of my solo album [from the song "Warmer Hands"]. Da-duh-do-do-da, I wanted to have that and the dan-do-dan-da-do-da, you know that would have sounded great with Yes. For some reason no one could understand it, so I saved it for later. I think some of the introduction to "Sound Chaser" was recorded at that time, not the solo. The Mini-Moog solo was recorded at Chris's house on Monday afternoon two weeks later. I did the solo, which I understand everyone was raving about. (TMI)

steve (1994): "Sound Chaser" is like this madman from hell . . . an indescribable mixture of Patrick's jazzy keyboards and my weird sort of flamenco electric, which I'm sure has never been done before and will probably never be done again! (TMI)

patrick (1995): Jon's flute was good on "Sound Chaser," it's a bit ear-bending, isn't it—that flute on "Sound Chaser"? It was too loud in the mix, though. (TMI)

steve (1980): To write a cadenza for the electric guitar with synthesizer and percussion accompaniment called for a short composition that the group could work from and inject into a song. In this excerpt from "Sound Chaser" the song goes at a high speed and the guitar has to lead off from this. Until the bass enters, the feeling is of tension and uncertainty, but from there on we devised a slightly "Hammer film" quality. (SHGP)

patrick (1995): I disagreed with Steve from day one on his choice of notes for the chords he wanted me to play to underline his guitar solo, a very aggressive guitar solo. I didn't like his choice of notes that he wanted me to play. I had a choice of notes that I liked much better, that I wanted to do, but he didn't want to learn it. It did no good to argue. (TMI)

alan (1994): We used to open the show with "Sound Chaser," but unfortunately it would take two or three songs for the band to settle down to any good tempo to perform because it was so fast. It was a dynamic, racy piece of music that had lots of tempo changes within it. So you really got on stage and that adrenaline you've got is usually let out in the first number. . . . It's the collective unit that is playing the tempo. And if one guy is playing fast, then everyone has to keep up.

In the intro I play in a different tempo than the band [Alan is playing in 4/4 and everyone else is in 5/4] and then we end up all together. A lot of Yes music from that era and prior to that were worked out mathematically, where we'd say this number of bars at that tempo goes into this number of bars at this tempo and we'll meet at this point. So we'll do so many of these and you'll do so many of them and we'll end up at this point. And that's how it was worked out. But that was the secret to some of those things was to have wild excursions by yourself musically and then end up at a point where you met everyone else. (TMI)

"TO BE OVER"

jon (1975): It's strong in content, but mellow in overall attitude. It's about how you should look after yourself when things go wrong. Steve and I wrote the introduction. Steve wrote a very beautiful drifting lament—he's got into using a steel guitar—I wrote the lyrics, and we all did the finale. (C)

steve (1975): I'd say something like "We go floating down the river," and Jon would change that to "We go drifting down the calming streams." And there were my words "She won't know what it means to me." Jon changed that to "To be over we will be." So Jon with his creativity disguised it into something that you have to consider to be over. It was a much broader lyrical statement. (MM)

(1994): I was in my studio and I saw some quarter-inch tape that I hadn't looked at and I saw "To Be Over" [written on the box] and I thought, "I'll put this one on." Pretty big-time in the studio and it sort of went through me, BOOM! Jesus, what kind of band was that, you know? How did we do that stuff? It's just remarkable. (TMI)

patrick (1995): I remember writing the counterpoint solo down on paper, because there was no more space for me to just improvise. There is a keyboard counterpoint solo that I play with different synthesizers . . . because I wanted to blend with Steve's guitar and Chris's bass and there was all kinds of elements and pauses and silences which made it in a way extremely contrived. I treated it exactly like a fugue, a classical fugue. Although it doesn't sound as baroque as it could have, given less modern harmonies, it is really structured like a fugue. I wrote it overnight and sweated quite a lot over it. It took me several hours to write it all on paper. (TMI)

alan (1995): I don't really play guitar and I know only a minimal amount of chords on the guitar, but I used to mess around on it a lot. I just wanted to know about it. Some parts of Yes music were things I came up with rhythmically, just changing the chords and Steve latched on to it. Songs like "To Be Over." (TMI)

ON MAKING SOLO ALBUMS IN 1975

A group decision in 1975 led to the recording and release of solo albums from each member. It allowed everyone the chance to do a whole record exactly as they saw fit and to use some of the backlog of material that had accumulated among them.

chris (1977): Through making solo records we'd all learned a lot and had much more to bring back and feed to each other. It also made us all appreciate that it was probably more enjoyable playing together than doing a solo thing, which is definitely much harder work because you're in charge of it all and there isn't anyone to share it with. Going through those vibes brings you back together and gives you a sense of release—relief as well—and also a lot of knowledge has been gained. (GIG)

YESTERDAYS
FEBRUARY 1975

While the members of Yes worked on their solo albums Atlantic Records decided to put out *Yesterdays*, a compilation of *Yes* and *Time and a Word*. It helped to fill the time between the next Yes album and also allowed their wonderful cover version of the Simon and Garfunkel song "America" to see the light of day (it had previously only been available on the sampler album *Age of Atlantic* and as a severely edited single).

jon (1974): I got it together and tried to pick out tracks that represented the first two years of the band. It was very enjoyable listening to it all again. The first thing I remembered was the way I felt at the time in the studio. Especially the first one, which was like—an *album*! (MM)

"AMERICA"

jon (1975): The idea for the beginning of "America" came when I was walking past the kitchen door one day and heard Tony messing around with a phrase. I said, "Hold it!" (MM)

steve (1993): The guitar solo on this is definitely one of my favorites. That track showed us having a fun time, but it also showed that we could still interpret other people's music. We tried to get away from that when we dropped Stephen Still's "Everydays" and all the songs Yes used to do from other composers from our set list. Rick wasn't terribly interested in doing this track, so consequently Bill Bruford plays the Mellotron on the end, which is quite astounding. Yes didn't play a lot of straight-ahead things, and this was an opportunity to come up with something very lively and demonstrated how I was feeling about America—how much I'd taken from it, and what I could give back. (GS)

(1973): We worked on nothing else but "America" for a whole week, getting the tempos right. It's a lot of fun to play. The moods, range from the calm of the prairies and Grand Canyon to the confusion of New York. It's totally a group effort. (MM)

bill (1994): I remember playing wah-wah conga drums on that. Wha-ti-chy, wha-ti-chy. If you listen to it, you'll find it's conga drums going through a wah-wah. (TMI)

"LOOKING AROUND"
"TIME AND A WORD"
"SWEET DREAMS"
"THEN"
"SURVIVAL"
"ASTRAL TRAVELLER"
"DEAR FATHER"

GOING FOR THE ONE
RELEASED JULY 1977 (7/7/77!)

When it came time to record the next album, the group decided to do it in Switzerland for tax reasons. Within a month of rehearsals it became clear that there was a problem between Patrick Moraz and Yes. He was asked to leave and Rick Wakeman was brought in through their mutual manager Brian Lane to work as a session man for the album. But as the band played the songs with Rick it was obvious that the best thing for everyone would be for him to rejoin Yes. *Going for the One* is an exuberant record and it clearly captures the good times the band had in creating it.

ON PATRICK LEAVING

chris (1977): Certain musical things that are natural to an English band weren't natural to him. Obviously he had to be slightly contrived some of the time both as a personality and as a musician in order to fit in. We ended up with a hell of a lot of music that we'd taken to certain point and never actually rounded off. And then we had a few raps about it and at the end of the day it was agreed as much on Patrick's part as the rest of us—that he would be happier doing something on his own. Because he started to feel a bit restricted. (GIG)

patrick (1991): I eventually left Yes because it was like a big festival of egos. There was never any conference on what was artistically important. It was always economical. (K)

(1995): I was kind of gently eased out of Yes. I was too young in the business to know what was happening. The motivation, of course, was that Brian Lane wanted to have Rick Wakeman back in the band. He was managing Rick, and Rick was not happening as one would have thought, although he had two number-one albums, I think. *Journey to the Centre of the Earth* and *The Six Wives of Henry VIII* had been very well received and we thought he was going to be the biggest keyboard rock star since sliced bread and it was not really happening. I was not fired as such. But it clearly happened one afternoon of November 1976, we had written most of *Going for the One*'s parts and I was having increasing difficulty trying to express my own voice within the confines of the band and what I've called the festival of egos. Although maybe it might be argued by the other guys that I was not comprehending the depths of whatever. (TMI)

ON RICK REJOINING

rick (1977): To be perfectly honest I was very pissed off. This was what my feelings for the band were. This sort of music was what I feel Yes music is. And here I am, come over as a bloody session musician to do what I feel the band should be doing anyway. Chris Squire came over and said, "I like your ideas." I said, "Yeah, I'm really knocked out. I'm glad Yes are taking this path." He said, "Well, how would you feel about making it a bit more permanent?" I said, "Yeah, I'd be into that." So I went home, packed all my bags, and I've been here ever since.(GIG)

steve (1994): I was very excited when we got Rick Wakeman back into the band, because I felt he was a more colorful and therefore more suitable keyboardist for Yes. (SHGC)

chris (1977): Rick shouldn't have left in the first place. It was all a bit of a copout. He still could have carried on his solo things. It was silly of him to leave. Especially at a time when things could've been so good. But he had ego problems and his album did well and he didn't get off on *Topographic Oceans*. And because we were all a bit younger then, maybe it wasn't talked about in the right way. But who am I to talk? I've had my hang-ups too. (GIG)

jon (1977): The album is a kind of celebration, over the last two or three years we've been experimenting a lot and we're happy to have been given that chance. . . . If we wanted another *Tales* concept, we would have gone in that direction, but we needed to relax for a while—[and have] a little more laughing and jive. (C)

alan (1977): I feel a touch of lightheartedness now in the band, and that's not the way it's been the past two years. It's been all too serious sometimes. Rick brings that touch of humor back into the music. (RS)

(1994): It's got a lot of fun stamped all over it, that album. We spent about eight months in Switzerland because we were all doing tax years out of the country. We had a very memorable period there where we were all living in these Swiss chalets and being very European. We'd go skiing in the morning and play in the afternoons. We'd write until we were finished in the evening. We had a lot of great times. Rick was being his usual crazy self, keeping everyone laughing that whole time. And some great music came out of it. (TMI)

chris (1977): It is a spontaneous-sounding record with a lot of good feeling on it. Without being egotistical, I could foresee that feeling would make it through to the record and that people would listen to it and feel it as well. A clear emotion produces a successful record. (GIG)

steve (1993): *Going for the One* was a good rebirth of Yes at that time, to find its feet and really know what it wanted to do. And we made "Awaken" and "Turn of the Century." "Going for the One" itself is a dynamic piece of music, unlike anything we ever did. It's very underrated, or very underrequested and underplayed. (NFTE)

"GOING FOR THE ONE"

jon (1977): I wrote that song about two or three years ago, it's about sports. The catch line is "The truth of sport plays rings around you/ Going for the one." Part of the song is about horse racing and there's a little bit on a film I saw about going down the Grand Canyon river on one of those rubber dinghies and there's also a bit in there about the cosmic mind, which is something I think a lot of people have been getting into lately. (C)

"TURN OF THE CENTURY"

jon (1977): It was originally a short song that we developed. As we began to rehearse it, I started to think, "Let's try to musically tell the story without me singing it, and then when I do sing it, it'll sound even better." (C)

I wanted to get a story done about a sculptor who wanted to make a stone statue of his lady, who died during the winter. The story was triggered off by *La Bohème*, which is a great opera, and I wanted to develop the story to the point where the music would take over. The point of the story is that he puts all of his love into the statue and it comes to life. It is an old Greek tale, and in putting it to song I wanted to become much more of a storyteller. (MM)

steve (1991): One of my favorite things, that is still a treat for me to listen to, is the opening minutes of "Turn of the Century." (WS)

alan (1994): I wrote pretty much all of the chords for it and came up with the idea of the way the drums develop into the timpani in the end. It was a chord sequence I had and was playing and Jon said, "Keep playing that!" And he came up with this idea of "Turn of the Century" and then Steve . . . just enhanced and embellished those chords a little bit and made them a little more sophisticated in some areas. It's very funny, but some of the songs I do get involved in writing become kind of the hits of the stalwart fans, like "Turn of the Century," "Shoot High, Aim Low," things like that. Bits of "Wondrous Stories" and *Topographic*. (TMI)

"PARALLELS"

chris (1995): It's about a spiritual kind of love, basically. It was one of my general-messages-of-hope sort of songs. "Parallels" could have been on *Fish out of Water* [Chris's solo album]—it was one of the songs I was playing around with—but I ended up saving it. There's a juxtaposition of two styles in that song with the cathedral organ and a blues bass riff going on together. (TMI)

steve (1994): The song didn't have any guitar riffs at all to start with, nothing. . . . You create at times much more than just a guitar solo. You create a finishing off of a structure that really wasn't going anywhere, we were just playing away with something and the guitarist, the keyboardist, or the singer has the opportunity to do something with it. (TMI)

"WONDEROUS STORIES"

steve (1991): "Wonderous Stories" was part of Jon's Renaissance period, where he quite liked a classical sort feeling to things. More so than when we just interjected it with rock. It had a very classical framework. (YY)

jon (1977): It was a beautiful day in Switzerland. It was one of those days you want to remember for years afterwards. The words "Wonderous Stories" came into my head. It's an exuberant song.

It was about the joys of life, as opposed to the uptightedness of some aspects of life. Romantic stories from the past and future, really—a kind of dream sequence. (MM)

alan (1995): My contribution to "Wonderous Stories" was the idea on how the bass and drums come in on the really odd beats. (TMI)

"AWAKEN"

jon (1977): While I was in Switzerland I had a chance to read a book called *The Singer,* it's about this Star Song which is an ageless hymn that's sung every now and again and that inspired this song. It's also influenced by a book I read recently about the life of Rembrandt—that affected me quite significantly. I feel the song ends the whole *Topographic* relation of ideas. (C)

(1988): I was walking past Steve's room in a hotel and he was playing the lick, so I kind of jumped in. . . . I started to understand where it could go and I wanted to go into a musical harp section in the middle and dream the audience, sort of Vivaldi, which is very sort of heavenly and grand and very cosmic. I'm singing to the master of our existence and I think the lyrics are very, very strong. (ST)

(1991): There's that final instrumental part in "Awaken" where Rick's keyboards just soar and I just shut my eyes and let it take over me. When I open my eyes, I always look to the audience for the energy to sing that last part of the song. (WS)

steve (1977): The very beginning of the guitar solo was worked out in advance. It was originally going to be part of a solo guitar piece. When we were actually arranging "Awaken" the basic riff of that solo was first used on the demo, but intended for the beginning of the song. It was one of those things where it might have been in the song or it might have been deleted. When we change things around in the studio, I very often end up putting in the bits that've been taken out—not necessarily in their original form or location, though. (GP)

alan (1991): "Awaken" is very hard to play on stage. But played correctly, that song is amazing. (WS)

(1994): We recorded it in different sections, but we had the full piece in our minds. We had the image of what it was going to be. What drove us to the great ending section of that whole thing was the fact that Rick was playing the church organ in a church that was ten miles down the road and we were hooked up through telephone lines and stuff like that. There's a lot of great innovative stuff like that going on. It was interesting counting someone in who wasn't there.

The middle section wasn't improvised, it was all set up. I was actually playing all of that section in one studio by myself and Rick was in the other place and we did that whole thing down the telephone lines. (TMI)

rick (1978): [on recording the pipe organ parts over the telephone line!] We did it that way because that's the way things are done in Switzerland. On being together, they make the United States and England look like they're the darkest Africa. Their telephone lines are the highest fidelity you can imagine. They said, "What do you need a mobile for? All you do is rent a phone line for a day." So we rented a phone line. I put on the cans [headphones]; the guys put on their cans and one, two, three, four, away we went. It was great. The pipe organ was recorded direct into the studio. I listened back to it over the cans, drove back to the studio, cut a little overdub, and that was it. Finished! (K)

patrick (1995): I personally think I did write "Awaken." I never got credit for any of the music that appears on *Going for the One.* All of the tunes that appear on *Going for the One* had been contributed to by me as much as the other guys in the band. Now Rick came in and put his own flavor and his own keyboards and his organ parts from Vevey. I couldn't believe that they would go with that kind of sound and that kind of arrangement. . . . If one wants to analyze very seriously what is happening in my solo album called *Out in the Sun,* [in] the piece "Time for a Change," one will notice in the opening of the song . . . that's the chords and melodies I wanted for "Awaken" and this album came out before *Going for the One* anyway and it's my music. And if you compare the two, you will notice that it is the same music, the same chords. . . . Also, the big difference was the treatment of the cycle of fifths, which was pretty elementary for me. What I was proposing to the band was to go for the endless ascension, which is also a cycle of fifths, but treated differently, and you can hear it on my third album [*Patrick Moraz*] on "Temples of Joy." About fifteen minutes into the record there is a rising of chords which is a cycle of fifths and it's the treatment I would have given the end of "Awaken." (TMI)

steve (1981): [Patrick] helped to get the album going. But you see, the problem is, what was our choice? He didn't make it in the end. We couldn't make the record with him. We prepared some of the material, and we did try to lose as much as would be offensive to him, or to us, of his style. We did take a lot out. But what he's sensing, of course, is the familiarity. He knows this. He hears this music and he says, "I was there when we were writing this." But of course, what we did was take out his idea and put in another idea. We had already heard his idea. So in some ways it's a compliment to him that he still feels he's in there. There are a couple of references to Patrick's music in there. And we intended in all good faith to put on the album something about Patrick. But it's too late now. (R)

TORMATO
RELEASED OCTOBER 1978

Tormato is a bit of an uneven album, reflecting the uncertainty that plagued the group at the time. Yes rehearsed and recorded a number of songs, but the project just seemed to lack direction. Nevertheless, the In the Round tour was a smashing success, so much so that the band decided to tour in 1979 without an album to support!

jon (1994): *Tormato* was a bit of a mess! (S)
   I felt as a collective unit, as you can tell by the photograph [on the back cover], that we are all looking in different directions. It was my idea for the photograph that we should all wear dark glasses because we are all looking in so many different directions. (YM)

steve (1992): The last album we made in those ten years with Rick and Jon, *Tormato,* was rehearsed more in the recording studio than anywhere else because things were getting very strained and painful. This meant, in effect, that we rehearsed less and although *Tormato* doesn't suffer from dreadful arrangements we definitely lost the sense of production on it. Although "Madrigal" and "On the Silent Wings of Freedom" are okay, we had a flatter sound than usual. We were trying to produce ourselves and we sometimes paid the price. (GTM)

alan (1994): *Tormato* has never been my favorite album. It's really strange, but a lot of people in America really like *Tormato.* Especially doing clinics around San Francisco it seems as if people like that album in that part of the country. In fact I did one clinic where eighty percent of the albums I got asked to sign were *Tormato.* It's really strange. There's a couple of funny things on there that I didn't consider to be the best Yes music. (TMI)

rick (1978): On *Tormato,* I wrote about four of the nine tracks. Mostly with Jon. But there were some publishing disagreements and a few problems. Never believe credits on any album. They're all political. This album had most things straightened out. Everyone's in control of their own part, but on the other hand, no one was afraid to say, "Well, Jon, I think you should sing this part." Or "Steve, that's a bad guitar part." Tempers got frayed

Rick Wakeman, on Keytar, facing off with bassist Chris Squire.

Steve playing one of his favorite guitars, a Gibson ES 175.

sometimes, but that's normal. It always gets worked out in the end. I think Yes agrees on the music it should play, but mixes are another story. One man's mix is another man's poison. I would like to see a real high-quality production man come in and work on a couple of Yes tracks. Somebody like George Martin [of the Beatles]. (K)

steve (1981): On *Tormato* keyboards were in real conflict with me not so much in the notation, but in the sound. The Poly Moog and other things weren't sympathetic. (R)

(1993): It was the album where we took Rick's Birotron and he went to the loo while he was doing some overdubs, and while he was in the loo we took out all his eight-track cassettes (from the Birotron) and we put mine in: quadraphonic Seals And Crofts and all these old eight-track tapes. So he came back and he said, "Okay, let's carry on." When he pressed the keys down he went, "What the hell is this?" It was like "We may never pass this—we may never pass this—we may never pass this" . . . if only he had laughed, though; he got quite cross! (NFTE)

We'd stopped using Roger Dean for cover artwork—this was apparently done to give us a new visual direction. My feeling was that if it's working, don't turn it off. But a design company called Hipgnosis did the *Going for the One* and *Tormato* sleeves, and I must say I dislike both. My original idea had been to call this album Tor—I'd found a map of Dartmoor with Yes Tor on it and thought it would be a good idea to have a black and white shot of that on the cover. But for some reason Hipgnosis seemed to think that a squashed tomato was a much better idea. (GTRSP)

chris (1994): It has "Onward" on it so of course I like my song and . . . it's got "The Silent Wings of Freedom," right? There's some good stuff on that album. . . . It just seems to me like both Rick and Steve on that particular album were seeing which one could play more notes than the other one. That's kind of how the guitar and keyboard parts were constructed on most songs, it seems . . . but I think Alan and I played well on it. Yeah, it is a mixture of an album, but I guess I'm with the fans, there are things either that I love and things about it I'm not too keen on as well. (NFTE)

rick (1978): I'm very pleased with the last two albums the band has done, although there's room for improvement on them all. I'm glad of that. If there wasn't, there'd be no place to go. I think we all have to improve our method of recording. There is no doubt about it. We take too long and we don't make full use of our time. (K)

"Future Times"

alan (1994): "Future Times" was great on stage. If that was recorded live it would have been a lot better. I think just the way the album was recorded in the studio that it was never that great. (TMI)

jon (1994): The musical prophesy in "Future Times" is one that I was thinking about the other day. The island of Arabia surrounding Israel. They get more island-like. There isn't a unified Arabic consciousness anymore. (YM)

"REJOICE"
"DON'T KILL THE WHALE"

rick (1978): Chris came along with a sort of Bo Diddley song, and Jon wrote the words to it, because one morning we were reading about the slaughter of all the whales, and that hit us pretty hard—the unnecessary slaughter of animals, I think is a little over the top. So I started making a few funny sounds on the Moog, like the whale being hit by a harpoon up its rear end, things like that. And then Alan started doing the Bo Diddley rhythm— and the next thing you know, we were into the song. (C)

steve (1992): I usually improvise my fills in songs. "Don't Kill The Whale" from *Tormato* has some quite strange fills going on alongside the vocals. The guitar might be pretty odd, but that's really fairly typical of me— I would always try to do something a little different or a little sideways. (GTM)

chris (1980): I wrote the song with different lyrics and Jon decided to write those lyrics. I thought the sentiment was nice, but it didn't turn out to be quite what I expected. (I)

"MADRIGAL"

jon (1978): I said, "Why don't we try to write a madrigal?" Which is an old-English-folk-after-dinner-song. So Rick sat down at the piano and we just wrote it and recorded it. (ES)

"RELEASE, RELEASE"

alan (1994): I wrote "Release, Release" with Jon. That was my contribution to that album. We played it on stage four or five times, but it was such a powerhouse piece of music that everybody would be so out of breath . . . it was just too much. It was one of Jon's favorite tracks too. (TMI)

rick (1978): You know the cheering in the drum solo in "Release, Release"? All that is totally and utterly phony. I believe it was from an English football match. We put it in because the drum and guitar parts sounded a bit dry, so we added the crowd. I like it actually. It's quite a good vibe. (K)

alan (1978): We just cast the drums out. We put ADT [automatic double tracking] on the drums so they sound as if they were in a giant auditorium right in the middle of this tight rock 'n' roll song. It makes people think a little about what they listen to initially. (MD)

"ARRIVING UFO"

jon (1978): That came up around the time of *Star Wars* and *Close Encounters*. I've always been interested in UFOs and sci-fi. (MM)

"CIRCUS OF HEAVEN"

jon (1978): I got the idea from a book by Ray Bradbury I'd read about ten years ago. When I was writing it, I did it the way I remembered the book, I talked to my son about it and he enjoyed the story. (MM)

"ONWARD"

steve (1993): "Onward" is a nice piece, a nice song. (NFTE)

chris (1995): Originally I played it to everyone on piano and sung it and the arrangement evolved from that. I used Andrew Jackman to do the strings, the same guy who did the orchestrations on *Fish out of Water*. Steve came up with the staccato guitar part and I think Rick came up with the bass line on the synthesizer. (TMI)

"ON THE SILENT WINGS OF FREEDOM"

jon (1978): It's a good stage number and a good song on the album. It's kind of hard-hitting Yes music. (ES)

alan (1978): It's a whole bass/drum jam. We went into the studio and re-created the jam and then the song came out of it. But there's a theme that the song always returns to—the theme of the jam we got into. (MD)
(1995): I started playing this whole thing which was in four, but with threes in the bass drum against it and that's where the whole thing developed from. We were just jamming on it and then it turned into the song. (TMI)

ON JON ANDERSON AND RICK WAKEMAN LEAVING IN 1979

The Paris sessions from 1979 signify the serious problems that were brewing within the band. They had worked hard at rehearsing and recording albums and then touring all over the world with very little time off. Everyone was tired and their personalities were all so different that there was very little agreement on anything. It was always that way, but now they couldn't count on the music to pull them through. Also, there were ongoing financial difficulties to aggravate the situation that seemed to never get sorted out.

Yes started recording demos with producer Roy Thomas Baker in Paris and within weeks the project was put on hold. The material was weak and performed in a perfunctory way and the band decided to reconvene and start anew in London in the New Year. It was then that the idea of the split became clear: Jon Anderson and Rick Wakeman would leave Yes and the band would continue without them.

rick (1981): It all worked very well up until about 1979. That's when it really started falling apart. The problems were both internal and musical. Jon and I had formed a partnership of playing and writing and a way of working. We just felt we weren't getting any input at all from any other areas. Everything became a struggle. We ended up recording an album which we never finished, and what happened was we got halfway through . . . and it was like Jon and I met one day in Paris in a little café and just said, "We've both had enough." I mean the band's just run out of . . . we were digging into a gold mine that just had a few nuggets left. (R)

jon (1980): I'd written quite a lot of songs with Rick. I felt the songs were valid, but there was some question by the other members as to whether they were. I just happened to be very prolific. Whether it's good or bad is a judgment in itself. I tend to want to write a lot of music and the other members hadn't that intensity for themselves. They wanted to write as a group. But Yes never did write together. Things change. (C)

steve (1980): The straw that broke the camel's back was that Alan White broke his foot, so we had to stop the sessions. Otherwise we might have gone on trying to make things work. Jon was using the group as a vehicle for his own songs. We fought that. We felt to get the best out of the group was to have as many co-compositions as possible. Also, we considered Jon's songs too folk-oriented. (C)

chris (1980): There are always outside aggravations. People making stupid decisions, financial problems, and all that. You can always get over them if, musically, you're all going in the same direction. But there are other times . . . (HP)

DRAMA
RELEASED AUGUST 1980

Chris Squire, Steve Howe, and Alan White decided to continue under the banner of Yes. They had a great time rehearsing and recording as an extremely powerful rock trio, but fate intervened and produced the wildest Yes lineup yet. Trevor Horn and Geoff Downes (of the Buggles, also managed by Brian Lane) had written a song for Yes and submitted it to them in the hopes of it being included on the next Yes LP. They were asked to come down to the studio and help record a demo of the song with the band and almost immediately a chemistry between the two camps emerged. Yes decided to bring Horn and Downes into the fold and the resulting album, *Drama,* is a fine addition to the Yes catalog. The production in particular was the best it had been in years, partly due to Eddie Offord returning to record the backing tracks. Unfortunately, after the British leg of the Drama tour Trevor Horn decided he wanted to go back to record producing and left Yes without a lead singer. Early in 1981 Alan White and Chris Squire decided to work with Jimmy Page on the ill-fated "XYZ" project, while Steve Howe and Geoff Downes formed the band Asia. At this point in time Yes ceased to exist.

ON GEOFF DOWNES AND TREVOR HORN JOINING

trevor horn (1980): Chris said, "Why don't you join?" Then he asked us again. And we sat down and talked to him for about two hours. He said, "I really want you to join. I've got this feeling that it could be really

Trevor Horn (top) and
Geoff performing at
Madison Square Garden.
PHOTOS © 1978 BY R. W. KOSTURKO

good. And it's finished, it's over with Jon and Rick. It's just like the end of an era. It's not working anymore and whether you join or not, it won't stay together. But I really think it'll be good if you join." And of course I went through all the reasons against it. Because I knew that if I said yes, that I was going to have to take a lot of shit. I didn't really know if I wanted to take it. I knew that we'd end up on stage. I knew that I'd have to do Jon Anderson's songs. And I knew that however I did the Jon Anderson songs, whether I did them like Jon, unlike Jon . . . whatever I did, there would be no way I could win . . . in certain people's eyes. I just didn't know whether I wanted to go through all that shit. I didn't need to . . . but Chris said, "Look, the three of us are going in the studio with Eddie Offord. We're going to put down some tracks. Why don't you and Geoffrey come in for a couple of days and we'll record 'Fly From Here?' Maybe I'll sing. But you come in and do it. Do some work with us." And they went into the studio for a week or so and they did some backing tracks. On the second day of recording Steve came up and said, "Look, are you two guys going to join the band? Why don't you do it? Why don't we make an album?" So I said to Geoffrey, "Why don't we do it?" And he said, "Yeah, why don't we do it? Let's do it." I said, "You realize, though, Geoffrey, that if we say we'll do it, I'll end up on stage at Madison Square Garden in front of twenty thousand people one day as a result of this decision." So he said, "Come on, give it a try. It could be really great. What have we got to lose?" (R)

chris (1987): All through the seventies, we were a band that had various personnel changes. Then Jon and Rick weren't in the band anymore and Trevor Horn and Geoff Downes were. It was my idea to bring them in—by that time I was pretty much in charge of the band. We'd lost a singer and a keyboard player—and here was a singer and a keyboard player who'd just had a number-one single in every country in the world except America. This made me think these were the guys who could help! In a way it was a very interesting experience, and *Drama* actually has some pretty good things on it. But it was another rushed album. (GW)

steve (1992): Jon had a whole lot of lyrics that he had written in Barbados but we didn't like them and Rick wasn't interested in rehearsing as much as we thought we needed. In just a few weeks Alan, Chris, and I had played most of *Drama*—we were playing "Tempus Fugit" as a very powerful rock guitar trio and it worked okay! But when we heard the keyboards and the quirkiness of [the] Buggles we thought that would be far better for us—we needed some new blood that was quite different. At first Trevor said he couldn't replace Jon, but we said we didn't want it like that anyway. We were going to change the group—I would have liked to have changed even more. We had loads of songs and ideas and we just blasted into it without worrying about it much. UK audiences brought it home that some fans wanted Jon back, which put Trevor in a weird position. It was quite sad because Trevor wasn't really given a chance to find his own feet. (GTM)

trevor horn (1980): My initial reaction [to being asked to join Yes] was one of horror. I'd been a Yes fan for so long. It was such a wild idea, but Chris was very persuasive. (C)

geoff (1980): There was obviously a period of time where the guys in Yes and Trevor and I didn't know if things were going to work out. We were a package deal, so there was never really any question of there being an audition. We decided to have a trial period of a couple of weeks to see if it would work out, and if it didn't, no one would have lost a thing. But we found it worked, so we stuck with it. (K)

It's a bit frightening being in the position Trevor and I are in. It's like stepping into a legend. The Buggles thing was nice, and we plan to do more of that, but if anyone had told us a year ago that we'd be doing this . . . (R)

(1994) It was a very well titled album under the circumstances, because it seemed to swing from week to week into another apocalyptic nightmare. From the Paris sessions to Alan breaking his leg so he couldn't do the drums, then Anderson and Wakeman left and Yes started recording in London. Then they got myself and Trevor started working with them, then Eddie Offord was in and then out . . . he freaked out and left. Everybody was totally on the edge, you know?

I think Chris wanted to reestablish the more of the old sound, or what he considers to be the old sound of Yes. That's why he was so into the Hammond I wanted to play on the record and Mini-Moog and that sort of thing. He viewed it more as being the spirit of the early Yes . . . "the revitalized Yes with the original concept." It was a good experiment from my standpoint, that I had the opportunity of blending a lot of things that I had grown up with, the classic sort of keyboard sound with also the technology that I had started to build up, synths and that kind of thing. It was sort of a cross-breed, which is quite difficult to do in a group situation, but particularly a group so ethnic-sounding as Yes. There has always been the technological edge on it as well.

Steve is not a reader [of music], but I think he found me to explain things a lot better than Rick did. And I think also that I was sort of more amenable than Rick was, when it came to actually working with him. I think some of the previous versions of Yes had been, "That's the way I play it, therefore [that's the way] it is." Which can be okay for a time, but I think Steve was appreciative that there was some communication. I think we were very in tune. (TMI)

rick (1991): When *Drama* came out, with Trevor Horn and Geoff Downes, I publicly said, "I don't class this as a Yes album. This has nothing to do with Yes." And I was very wrong. I aimed that remark at Chris, to whom I have apologized and apologize again. Without *Drama,* there would not have been a *90125,* and there would have been no Trevor Rabin coming in to bring the band into the eighties with a whole new style of playing. *Drama* may have been a low-selling album, but boy, it was an important catalytic element as to what happened in the eighties. (K)

jon (1981): I felt Trevor [Horn] was put on the spot. It was a very difficult position to fill—not because of me. But to be put on a stage. He'd never really toured before. So it was going to be hard for him to hold an audience, to keep himself going and to push the band. (R)

alan (1994): Trevor Horn was never really a front man and he found it very hard to fill Jon's shoes, I suppose. I think he felt, not intimidated by it, but like he was more prone to being a producer instead of being a front guy of a band. (TMI)

trevor horn (1985): Joining Yes was one of those stupid things that you do sometimes. It was one of the two or three times in my life that I've done something that I knew was wrong. (MN)

peter (1991): I think my favorite Yes album after I left was *Drama*, because I like Trevor Horn's work a lot. (YHS)

geoff (1994): I still maintain the *Drama* album was a good album, it was a good Yes album. I think a lot of the Yes fans do appreciate it. Obviously there were the criticisms that were aimed at us, "It isn't really Yes, no one can take over from Jon Anderson." It wasn't such a bad situation from my standpoint, because I was the fourth Yes keyboard player, but Yes had never replaced a vocalist before. Just from an image standpoint, Trevor's image was totally unsuitable to the sort of iconoclastic Yes image of what a vocalist should be in that group, which is sort of esoteric, cosmic if you like, which is its hallmark. Trevor's image didn't fit into that at all. Having said that, I do think the record is a good record. I've heard from various sources that Jon Anderson doesn't really even sort of recognize it as being a Yes record.

[The problems] weren't so apparent when we were playing the big places in America like the Cow Palace and Madison Square Garden, because the group is almost larger than its individual identity in a way. It's more Yes is the package. Whereas I think when we came to Europe after that and we played in some of the smaller theaters, there was a very, very hostile reception towards Trevor. They were very critical in a lot of the papers too. And I don't think that Trevor wanted to do it either. I think he wanted to get back to being a man behind the controls as opposed to being in front of the screen. (TMI)

"MACHINE MESSIAH"

alan (1994): I wrote all of the stuff to "Machine Messiah"; that was my baby on that album. All of the dudoda-dudoda stuff I wrote. So I had a good understanding of what that piece of music was. In fact Chris still curses me to this day for coming up with it. He said, "I can't play that on guitar—it's a keyboard lick!" And I said, "No, just keep practicing it!" and he did master it. I think he was gratified in the end that I kept pushing him into learning it, because it's a good piece. . . . It was just a powerhouse piece of music and it was great on stage too. (TMI)

geoff (1994): I think that was probably the most integrated composition on the *Drama* album from myself and Trevor's side and the old Yes side, if you like. That seemed to encapsulate the mixture of what the Buggles were about and what Yes were about as well. And I think that [song] probably for me is really the most interesting track on the album, because it has all of the different mood changes in it and it's pretty heavy. It's quite a heavy statement and I think Trevor's lyric writing was pretty perceptive. The machine messiah is a great concept, I think anyway. That song was more the direction that we should have gone in. (TMI)

trevor horn (1980): We wrote "Machine Messiah" in a day. We were pretty pleased with it. I had the tune for the first verse and they had the really heavy part. They played it to us and we put the two together. They also had the instrumental section and I had that quiet "Machine, Machine Messiah" part. (R)

I don't think the lyrics are that much different in terms of the surreal flavor of all the Yes lyrics from previous songs. I think, though, that they have a much more modern flavor. (SDS)

alan (1994): Eddie Offord did the backing tracks, but he didn't finish the songs off. All of the drum sounds came from Eddie Offord and we used the Townhouse Studios in London, which is the same place where Phil Collins recorded his famous drum sound. It's called the Stone Room. It's just basically a really vibey drum room and the way they got that sound was there was an old microphone, which was a talk-back microphone hanging from the ceiling, and they left it on by mistake one day. It was mixed into the drum sound and everyone went, "Wow, what a great sound." And that's why everyone went back to that room. (TMI)

"MAN IN A WHITE CAR"

geoff (1994): The music was by me, the lyrics were all Trevor. I think he wrote it originally about Gary Numan. He used to drive a white Stingray that he got as a present from his record company. And Trevor saw him driving along one day and he wrote the song about it. Gary Numan used to have this painted white face . . . "Move like a ghost on the skyline." That was the image of Gary Numan driving in this white car. (TMI)

[All of the instrument sounds came from Downes's Fairlight keyboard.]

"DOES IT REALLY HAPPEN?"

chris (1995): We had been working on this one as a trio and then Trevor and Geoff came along and we added to it. I remember Trevor Horn and I writing the lyrics to that song. (TMI)

geoff (1994): That was Chris, really, I think. That was actually a track that they already had, apart from the middle section, I think, and the chords that go against that. It had that basic groove. (TMI)

alan (1994): I did the drum pattern, da-do-da-do-dang-dang, that led to the direction of what the music was. Sometimes I come up with things rhythmically that would lead the music in another direction on some of those things. (TMI)

"INTO THE LENS"

alan (1991): "Into the Lens" was written mainly by Trevor Horn and conceived in the period of time when he joined Yes. (YGVH)

geoff (1994): I think the Yes version is a more interesting arrangement [than the Buggles version], but I think the song was pretty much as it was. I don't think it changed really that much. There were obviously a few extrapolations and arrangement embellishments, but otherwise I don't see the Buggles version being that different a song. I think it was a bit confusing, because we had a finished article before we had met them and Chris really liked the song, but obviously he wanted to turn it into being more of a Yes-like song. (TMI)

"RUN THROUGH THE LIGHT"

steve (1992): I'm in the background being very melancholy with the Les Paul. I think it's a really good guitar to get bluesy on—just because I don't play a lot of blues guitar doesn't mean that I haven't or I don't want to, I just got it out of my system in the Syndicats. (GTM)

geoff (1994): I think it was originally one of Chris's ideas, the song itself. Chris actually played Clavinet on it, because he had the feel for it. He had written it around the Clavinet. Trevor also played the bass, but I didn't play the guitar on that! (TMI)

trevor horn (1980): Chris said, "Why don't you play bass on track and I'll play piano." I didn't particularly want to play bass on the album and it took me awhile to get the part together for "Run Through the Light." I didn't quite know what to play on it. After I'd worked on it a bit somebody told me it was in 6/4 and I said, "No wonder I'm finding it hard to play the bass part." Chris came into the studio and more or less produced it. I kept saying to Chris, "Why don't you play it? You're the bass player in this band!" But he was really determined that I do it and one day we spent twelve hours playing and working out the final bass part. (R)

"TEMPUS FUGIT"

steve (1991): The title of it, "Time Flies" [in Latin], was a bit of a send-up on Chris, because he has a lot of trouble getting to places on time. (YGVH)

chris (1991): It's slightly punky, strangely enough. It was 1979 when we did it . . . it was definitely in the spirit of the times. (YGVH)

geoff (1994): This was another one they were working on as a trio, but there were no real chord structures built up. It was more riffs with monophonic lines. Of course there were no lyrics or title. Most of their songs were in that condition. They were kind of a selection of riffs, really. (TMI)

trevor (1980): What really got me was the first time we played "Tempus Fugit" [live] and everybody stood up at the end of it and went bananas. I felt great. Somebody had mentioned that it was odd to keep saying yes in a song because it was something Yes had never done before. But I thought, "What the hell, we'll do it. Maybe it'll be good." And when we hit that high part in the song, "From the moment you tell me . . . Yes," everyone went wild. I remember singing that on stage . . . "If we wait for an answer," the crowd was getting really up and I thought, "It's going to work." Because everyone liked it and it was a new song. To get that sort of high from a new song, which was the same sort of high we were getting from doing "And You and I," was really great. It sort of justified us being there. (R)

ON THE END OF YES (IN 1981)

steve (1982): Come the beginning of 1981, nobody was really sure of the destiny of Yes. We had a meeting and the egg sort of cracked on the floor and it ended up that really only Geoff and I were sitting there saying, "Well, I think I'm still in Yes. I haven't left. I haven't been fired or axed by anybody." So that's what happened. Geoff and I sort of felt, "Well, can we carry on Yes?" And I thought, "God, I've been doing this for a long time . . . trying to work out how the group continues." . . . I said, "No, Geoff, you do the Buggles, and I'm going to take a short break." But within a couple of weeks I'd realized we couldn't resurrect this, we couldn't piece this back together. It's really cracked wide open. So we started on the next project. (R)

YESSHOWS
RELEASED DECEMBER 1980

In the summer of 1979, Chris Squire holed up in his home studio with hours of Yes concert tapes to make the selections for this album. Demo mixes were made and a Roger Dean sleeve was created for the project before it was shelved by the band (because they couldn't agree on which songs to be used and the mixes). After Yes was put on ice, Atlantic Records went looking to see what suitable Yes product was about and gave the go-ahead to have *Yesshows* released.

steve (1982): It was released for the wrong reason. It was stopped for the right reason when it could have come out before. We wanted to refine it and we wanted to make it into a triple. I strongly objected to some of the edits on the album. But the way things were, they wanted a certain shock value. A certain person thought it was marvelous. Anyway, in the end the person who did it didn't want it coming out after all.

There were two main dreams in Yes—to get certain pieces of music recorded live, that were really strong. Like side four of *Topographic Oceans* and "Gates of Delirium." Of course, when we did record them, they got mixed by Chris. So anyway, the album was supposed to live up to this idea of getting those numbers down. And "Gates" wasn't a good mix at all. (R)

chris (1995): I think it's one of our best albums, actually. I can say that maybe because I was producing it, I suppose. (TMI)

rick (1981): [on the release of *Yesshows*] I think it's disgraceful. We recorded some of the dates and there were enough tapes to produce a "live album. . . ." We always thought the group was better live than on record. We're dreadfully clinical in the studio; we're well aware of it and the music suffers from it. Chris mixed some stuff, which was good, but nothing exciting. The next thing I knew was that somebody gave me a copy of *Yesshows*, and it turned out to be those horrible demo mixes. I can't do anything about it, but nobody told us it was coming out. (MR)

jon (1982): They put out the live album, which was a disaster, to me. They were just tracks put together. It just wasn't a communal work. (R)

alan (1994): I don't mind *Yesshows* coming out. It's just a part of the music business, where people just try to capitalize on certain successes. So you have to live with that kind of thing, you can't really do anything about it. There's no sense in getting upset about things like that. (TMI)

patrick (1995): It's not that bad. (TMI)

"PARALLELS"
"TIME AND A WORD"
"GOING FOR THE ONE"
"THE GATES OF DELIRIUM"

chris (1995): When we originally recorded in 1974 it was so much in sections; we didn't even know what the end of the song was when we started it. When we came to the studio each day we just did the next new bit, it was never played as a piece of music from beginning to end until it was all edited together. I thought it was a little bit scrappy, to be honest, when we finished the album. But after we'd played it on stage I was happy to put that version on the *Yesshows* album, because by then it had taken on an identity. You could tell when we were playing the beginning that we knew where we were going! (TMI)

patrick (1995): It's okay, but we've done better than that. I've heard hundreds of better versions of that song than the one that appeared on *Yesshows*. It's representative, but it's not really state of the art and that's what I regret. (TMI)

alan (1995): I would personally like to play "The Gates of Delirium" again. That on stage was just a great number and there's not really any footage of it or a great recording of it. If we played it now we'd make it more nineties and people would probably get quite blown away by it. (TMI)

"DON'T KILL THE WHALE"
"RITUAL"

patrick (1995): I think "Ritual" is quite good, but it's too bad that they broke it up. I wish that there was not so much bass in the mix. I mean there's a lot of bass, no? It's not quite as crisp as I remember it to be on stage, because we had some really powerful monitors. (TMI)

"WONDEROUS STORIES"

90125
RELEASED NOVEMBER 1983

After the XYZ project fell apart, Alan White and Chris Squire kept working together. They released a wonderful single, "Run with the Fox," and began casting about for members to create a new band. Trevor Rabin (of Rabbitt), a triple-threat musician—multi-instrumentalist, composer, producer—was given a call to come and audition for the duo. They found there was a connection between them and brought Tony Kaye into the project as their keyboardist. The band rehearsed for several months before securing a deal under the name of Cinema and began working on their album with none other than Trevor Horn producing. As the record neared completion there was pressure from different sources to have a lead singer join the band. The person asked to fill the position turned out to be Jon Anderson, and it now made sense to call the band Yes. The resulting album, *90125*, was a huge success all around the world and the lead-off song "Owner of a Lonely Heart," was a number-one single, making Yes's comeback one of the most incredible in all of rock history.

chris (1987): I was suspicious of Trevor when I was first made aware of him. It was about '79, and the manager I had at the time, Brian Lane, gave me this tape and said, "Here, you know what you should do . . . ?" He was like this scheming-manager-type guy who would secretly go to every guy in the band and just sound everyone out until he got some sort of reaction. So I was a little suspicious of Trevor for that reason. I heard this tape that Brian had given me and the guy played and sang everything on it and it sounded just like the last Foreigner album prior to that time, whatever it was. So I thought, "Who is this guy? What does he actually do?" But he did it all very well—he could sing like Lou Gramm and he could play like any guitarist I'd ever heard, more or less. And produce his records and play drums! So I thought, well, the guy is obviously a bit of a clever dick—but what is he really saying? But when I actually met him, we got on really well. In fact, the first time he came over to London to talk about forming this new band, we had this awful jam. We didn't really play very well at all, but we actually liked each other, so we didn't really care. (GW)

trevor rabin (1994): I was looking for a record deal. I had written most of the *90125* album and I wanted to record. I got some responses from various record companies, Arista included, that stated the stuff was far too left-field and wouldn't make it in the market today. Consequently it became a number-one album. But how I went about it was I sent tapes out and one bit of interest came from Atlantic Records. It came in the way of, "We've got a couple of bands together. Chris Squire and Alan White, and Jack Bruce and Keith Emerson." So there were two options. From a selfish point of view, I thought, "What I really need is a great rhythm section." So I got together with Chris and Alan. To cut a long story short, we then decided to contact Tony Kaye. I'd played all the keyboards on my demos, but who was going to play the stuff live? He came over, we got on well, and that consequently turned into the *90125* lineup, less Jon. The band was called Cinema, and there was never any intention to call it Yes. At the last minute, Chris happened to play Jon a track at a party or something, Jon loved it, and came in to sing on a couple of tracks—which I was very excited about. I listened to it and thought, "God, it sounds amazing." So we asked if he would like to join the band, which he did. (K)

(1995): What we did on *90125* based on the demos I had written was so different from *Close to the Edge* or *Fragile*. If I knew that it was going to turn into a Yes album I would have done things a bit differently; more from my orchestral point of view. But when I first met Chris and Alan we didn't even talk about that—I was a guitarist who wrote and sang.

I think it is important to remember that "Owner" was Yes's only number one and *90125* was their most successful album and was well-received by the most skeptical and cynical of critics. However, it has always been frustrating to me to be perceived as the guy who just writes the hit songs. Since the album and the single were so successful they have almost been equated with commercialism, rather than people just liking the album and buying it. You get a lot of credibility when things don't sell. (TMI)

(1985): It was a difficult album because nothing was left untouched. A lot of times you think, "Well that'll do." But not here. Every time someone wanted to do that, someone else would say, "No bullshit." And he's [Trevor Horn] a very demanding producer, which is great. It's the way I work. And besides guitar and vocals, I really enjoyed doing keyboards with him. After Tony had gone back to L.A. I did a lot of keyboards. And it was great fun working with him. (R)

tony (1985): We knew that the album would have to be somewhat simple. So we kept it very dimensionally sparse. We wanted it to be more modern-sounding; we wanted to appeal to an audience that the Police or the new Genesis would appeal to. It couldn't just be old Yes and the same old dirge, yet at the same time we knew that it mustn't sound like Styx or Journey, those kinds of American bands with vague English roots. (K)

alan (1991): The enthusiasm that we all felt for Cinema was really what you were listening to when you heard *90125*. We spent eight months rehearsing all of that material. A lot of the success of that album came from dedication to a new kind of sound. (YY)

steve (1988): When I first heard the *90125* one—when I heard that, I really kind of freaked out. You know what I mean. I kind of freaked out and said, "It's not Yes," that was my reaction, "This isn't Yes." I could hear Jon a bit, and I hear Chris, which often fundamentally is very Yes, but I just didn't feel that same kind of . . . the quality wasn't missing because I was missing, it was missing because in a way the kind of work that we've done couldn't be repeated. And therefore, I thought, "Oh, well, that's change." But as the record grew into excess and excessive, in a way, it grew a little bit with me. I became less strict and kind of turning a blind eye to it and I got a little more involved. (YM)

bill (1985): It's very good pop. I don't have any other association or feeling for it. I think they were a very good pop group at the time and are a very good pop group now. (R)

rick (1992): It was interesting when the band changed direction and Trevor joined and *90125* came out, which was a great album, great stuff, great songs—an important album, as important as *Fragile*. The thing is at that time it needed something like that, of importance. Whichever you think is the definitive Yes lineup, it was still a bloody important album. You see everyone said then that the music Yes did in the seventies was dead. What came along? The gap was filled by Marillion, perfectly, thank you very much! Fish [Marillion's lead singer at the time] is a good friend of mine and he said to me, "This is crazy, Yes are our idols. If they're not gonna do that any-more, well, we're gonna carry on doing it." You should learn from these lessons. (TR)

geoff (1994): The *90125* album obviously is interrelated in way be-cause of their work with Trevor [Horn] on that. It was quite a milestone, really, for them. The music really didn't reflect the music of Yes prior to that, I think. Largely because it was the first album that Steve didn't play on. And I think *90125* kind of sparked off quite a division, in the following—the fans of the group. In a way it didn't really have the spirit of the original concept, which is not necessarily a bad thing. (TMI)

"OWNER OF A LONELY HEART"

trevor rabin (1991): I wrote the bass line of it, which is the key to the song or the foundation of the song . . . when I was on the toilet. I have a great sound in the toilet and I always sing in the toilet. And it was a par-ticularly long visit and so I wrote the bass line and I came up with the lyric, "Owner of a Lonely Heart." It just developed from there. (YGVH)

chris (1987): Ahmet Ertegun came down to the studio and said, "We have to have a hit single this time. You have to work on it. It is your responsibility, Chris, to make sure it happens." And fortunately, we did it.

What I learned from "Owner" is the wonderful thing of people going, "Is that Yes? Really?" I like that. It's especially good for all the fans who stuck with Yes for the right reasons—people who'd been written off by others who'd say, "Oh, he's into that old Yes shit." When "Owner" came out, those same people could finally say, "Have you heard my band's new single?" (GW)

(1985): Trevor Rabin wrote it. I wrote the bridge section to replace his original bridge. Trevor Horn had this wacky idea of sampling all the James Brown horns onto the Fairlight. . . . He sampled the thirteenth chord and Alan White played it on the Fairlight. (G)

trevor rabin (1987): The Roland Pedal Library has some sounds of me, "Trevor Raven," it says, and when I saw that, I thought, what a great compliment. But then I opened it up and it had the setting for "Owner." Ridiculous. God forbid that's my style. Imagine being stuck with that as your style—it's a pretty peculiar sound. (GW)

Steve Howe unplugged.

Chris and Jon flash a rare smile on the Big Generator tour.

trevor horn (1985): It was imperative, coming back after such a load of shit, that Yes have a single. I would have killed to get that. That song was our best shot, so I made sure that it was as right as I could get it. (MN)

trevor rabin (1995): There's actually a couple of words on "Owner" where Jon had left the country and Trevor Horn wasn't happy with them. And I redid the words sounding like Jon. If you go back and listen to it I'm sure you can find them. (TMI)

tony (1985): I tried to make sounds that were either percussive or very dynamic, so that you could bring them out in the mix, as opposed to pad them where vocals were going to be. That was very much the approach to "Owner of a Lonely Heart." (K)

bill (1994): I didn't hear any Yes material at all after *Close to the Edge* until *ABWH* [*Anderson Bruford Wakeman Howe*], with the sole exception of "Owner of a Lonely Heart." Which was impossible to avoid and I liked it a lot. I thought it was really, really good. I didn't think it could be Yes, I thought it had to be Trevor Horn. It was one guy's vision, that song. It was very good. It's been a long slow decline in the seventies (for Yes music) with the sole exception of "Owner of a Lonely Heart." But good things can't go on forever and I think Yes had a naturally exciting six years probably and then after that it got a bit slow, but that's a long life span for a musical group and people sitting in each other's pockets. They should have all split up and done something fresh. (TMI)

geoff (1994): I don't think, really, that Yes were really about "Owner of a Lonely Heart," even though it was their most commercial single. In a way it can cause an amount of destruction in a group, because of the constraints of the commercial end of the business. You know, "I don't hear an 'Owner of a Lonely Heart' on this record!" I think subsequent Yes records have suffered from the "Owner of a Lonely Heart" legacy. Not necessarily in the fans' eyes, but in the record company eyes and the perception of the general public that aren't really fans. They bought that record for "Owner of a Lonely Heart" and then you come out with something that doesn't fit that bill on *Big Generator* and everyone's tearing their hair out because it's a commercial disaster. I have been in that position a few times in Asia with the song "Heat of the Moment." You lay a bit of a sidewinder in your career by having a very successful hit record. I know it sounds sort of converse, but in the context of a respected musical band like Yes or Asia, it can be a double-edged sword; a hit record like that . . . I think it virtually happens every time everyone has a big hit record, it's quite difficult to take stock of that and sustain a career out of it. Sometimes it's good just staying a musician, because once you think you're catering to people's tastes it's a big mistake. You sacrifice your integrity and it doesn't mean you're going to be successful. You could spend six months on a record to please some A&R guy and you might get a bullet the day before your record comes out. (TMI)

"HOLD ON"

trevor rabin (1985): "Hold On" was called "Moving In." "Hold On" was two songs I'd written and they were both in the same tempo. So we kept the chorus from "Hold On" and we used the verses from "Moving In." (R)

(1995): I remember one show we did where the combination of Chris and Alan playing during the guitar solo at the end . . . actually gave me a lump in my throat. I thought, "This is about as good as it gets." (TMI)

"IT CAN HAPPEN"

chris (1995): I wrote that one on the piano. Trevor came up with that intro part to go with my original piano chords. We got to rehearsing it as a band and did it for quite a long time before we recorded it for *90125*. (TMI)

"CHANGES"

alan (1994): I wrote the lick at the beginning of "Changes." Trevor wrote the song and I wrote the bit at the beginning. I was in a mall in Japan and I heard the dun-dun-dun-da-dun-da-dun-da incessantly forever and it's the only piece they used. So I kept saying to one of the managers, "You know, I should be getting royalties for this!" So it came up and I said to Trevor, "You know I wrote the beginning [to "Changes"]," and he said, "Oh, I forgot about that, you did, didn't you!" (TMI)

trevor rabin (1995): The lyric I wrote in a very depressed time. I had just moved to America and had these thoughts of doing wonderful things. I was with Geffen Records on a development deal and they just wanted me to form a rock 'n' roll band and I was really trying to do something different. In a meeting I went to they played Foreigner to me and they said, "You've got to start writing stuff more like Foreigner." I said, "I'm not going to, but thanks anyway." I thought I'm going through all of these changes, it's very strange. And consequently I think that's when that song started coming to me. It's kind of a melancholy song. (TMI)

"CINEMA"

[This was the opening of a twenty-minute song called "Time," which was never released. "Cinema" won the 1984 Grammy award for Best Rock Instrumental.]

"LEAVE IT"

trevor rabin (1991): Chris and I wrote the song together. He wrote the bass line and I put the melody on top. We went to record it and couldn't get a drum sound at all. It was just hopeless in the studio we were at, so we started putting on vocals first, saying we'd put the drums on afterward. And so really because the emphasis was not on getting a rhythm thing going, I just started thinking vocal-arrangement-wise. I said we should do this as a major a cappella type of thing, use the voices as instruments. And so that's what happened. (YGVH)

(1995): After we had recorded these vocals the engineer wiped the time code, so we couldn't sync up everything. So I sat up in the studio for two or three days transferring all the vocal parts onto a Synclavier, so I could play it back in. I played all the vocals back into the song and we decided that it was fine, but it didn't feel completely right. So we redid the whole thing on top of the Synclavier stuff. It took weeks to redo all the vocals! (TMI)

"OUR SONG"

alan (1995): I came up with the original line at the beginning of the song, that was my contribution to that song. (TMI)

trevor rabin (1995): If you listen to the song "Take It Easy," the chorus of that—its chord structure is very similar to "Our Song." It was kind of borrowed for "Our Song." However, the rhythm of it is totally different. The main verse riff is something that we got together in rehearsal in the Cinema days. (TMI)

"CITY OF LOVE"

trevor rabin (1995): I got a call from Foreigner—they needed a keyboard player for a tour and would I be interested? So I thought while I'm trying to get a deal I may as well go on the road—it's certainly better than playing bar mitzvahs or teaching. I went to New York for a rehearsal with the band and I was dropped off by a cab driver. I'd never been to this area before and was very naive to New York and I was taken to the wrong address, which ended up being in Harlem! I asked the cab driver where the address was and he pointed to it and said, "I ain't driving down there!" I just sort of obliviously walked through and I asked some shady-looking guy at this street corner where the address was. Now that I think about it, he was looking at me thinking, "I wonder what I can get from him?" Something must have been on my side because no one did anything to me and eventually I got back to reasonable humanity—I caught a cab to the correct address. That event inspired "City of Love." When I got back to L.A. I thought, "God, had I known where I was—I would have been terrified!" I started writing this guonk, guonk . . . this ominous kind of thing. It came very easily and this idea of waiting for the night to come was that the derelicts came out of the sewers at nighttime to be thugs. Later Jon put his slant on it which made it more interesting. (TMI)

"HEARTS"

trevor rabin (1995): I had written the chorus and bridge about two months before I met up with Chris and Alan. Tony Kaye wrote the intro riff and I wrote the melody on top of that. Jon was responsible for the counter-melody over it, "See me . . ." It was a collaboration all the way around. I know Jon has a real soft spot for that song, it creeps up in a lot of his solo projects. I don't mind, keep those checks rolling! (TMI)

BIG GENERATOR
RELEASED SEPTEMBER 1987

The many production credits and recording studios on the *Big Generator* album sleeve give some idea of how difficult it was to put it together. There was a lot of friction on the sessions between everyone over the direction of the album and the performance of the songs. It took a very long time to sort it all out and after Yes had completed touring for *Big Generator,* Jon Anderson decided to leave the band.

jon (1989): It was a very difficult album to record. There was no clear direction. That's why it took so long and took a lot of energy out of everybody. It didn't breathe the clear air that we all expected it to. It was a very exciting album to perform. It was just one of those things. I don't want to do that again! (YM)

trevor rabin (1987): Before we started we thought a lot about *Abbey Road* as a model. In the sense that, if we come up with an idea, why pressure ourselves into making it a song? Just have it there. If you can't come up with a chorus, don't throw it out because it's not a complete song and don't put a bad chorus around it; just leave the chorus out. So it evolved into an album with long songs, ranging from four to nine and a half minutes.

[Trevor Horn] was pulling it one direction, us in the other, and nothing ever got sorted out. We had a lot of trouble, and eventually—speaking for myself, but I think everyone felt this way—enough was enough.

The work I was most happy with was when I went in on a Sunday with nobody there and I was able to focus on what I was doing. So eventually I just said, "Stop. Let's go back to L.A." (GW)

chris (1987): I realized—but certain other people didn't—that going to Italy to save money was the start of doing it wrong. Inevitably when you try to do anything to save money, it ends up that because it's cheaper it's not the best place to be—and therefore you end up redoing it somewhere else. So we had to redo stuff in London, and other people weren't happy with Trevor Horn doing it either, so we ended up doing it in L.A.! The most sensible thing in the world would've been if we'd never left here in the first place; then the album would've been finished a year ago. (GW)

trevor rabin (1995): The reason I suggested going to Italy was I felt the band really needed to bond together. People were living in different places in the world and I thought we should almost be forced to be together to create music. This place in Italy was a luxurious castle, a beautiful old place for us to record.

We weren't going there to save money, the reason for going was purely because I felt it would bind us, or bond us together. But it turned out that there was too much partying going on and we didn't click and Trevor Horn said rightly after three months, "This is not working here. Let's get back to London." (TMI)

chris (1992): There was a lot of strange technical arguments going on between engineers and producers. . . . I think there was more time spent in

JON ANDERSON

PHOTO CREDIT: LISA TANNER

CHRIS SQUIRE

PHOTO CREDIT: LISA TANNER

BILL BRUFORD

TONY KAYE

STEVE HOWE

RICK WAKEMAN

TREVOR RABIN

ALAN WHITE

**THE TALES FROM
TOPOGRAPHIC OCEANS TOUR**
© ROBERT ELLIS/ REPFOTO LONDON

A CURTAIN CALL
PHOTO CREDIT: J. RISTORI

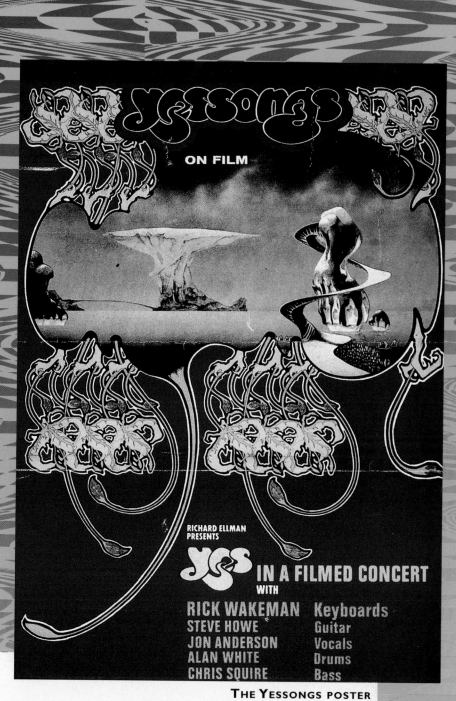

THE YESSONGS POSTER

THE EIGHT-MAN SUPERGROUP

ON THE UNION TOUR

control rooms discussing if anyone had tried the new "XR-3000Z+7 Discombobulator" than actually working on the music. There was tons of that going on. (YM)

trevor rabin (1990): It worked well for me because Chris and Jon don't get on well at all—this is the first time I've said this in an interview, but it's the truth—so it created a great vacuum for me to work in because there was all this friction going on. But I don't blame Jon for leaving because it got to the point where it was a little contrived and starting not to work. (WS)

"RHYTHM OF LOVE"

trevor rabin (1991): The idea behind that was just sex, you know, the rhythm of love. I thought we've been cheeky enough with Yes by doing a song like "Owner of a Lonely Heart," pushing away from the cosmic lyrics we all know. I thought it would be a nice little tease to have a sex lyric in. (YGVH)

jon (1988): The group wanted that kind of chorus. I wasn't so sure, but in some ways it was a group thing. It was a Trevor Rabin song, but lyrically it needed to be fashioned a little bit so we had a few lyrics changed, but it's more of a group identity sort of song. You know, "Rock 'n' roll, let's get down, boogie." (ST)

"BIG GENERATOR"

chris (1991): I wrote the riff for the song "Big Generator" along with Trevor Rabin. In a way the song came out of the tuning of my five-string bass, the instrument created the song in this case rather than the other way around. (CSV)

trevor rabin (1987): "Big Generator" was a song that I started playing and Alan joined in and I wrote a song around it. Tony wrote some chords for the verses . . . there's a lot of involvement from everyone. (MAT)

alan (1994): We were playing the song and it was turning out to be a pretty heavy rock 'n' roll song. And I thought we needed to put some Yes stamps in it. We were just going through the motions of recording the song and I said, "Look when we get to this section, you guys just keep on playing and don't listen to what I'm doing." This was the original way we were doing it. So they kept playing and I just stopped and started doing this kind of thing—like the drummer fell off his stool and then got back on trying to catch up the beat. Playing very slowly and then faster and faster on the snare drum and then I was back in time. But when I got back in time I reversed the beat around backwards so I came in with the bass drum on two and four instead of one and three. So that's the way we actually recorded it, but then when I got to the studio the next day Trevor had counted how many notes there were and had worked out a whole guitar lick that went with it! And they had cut out all of the backing and wiped it. They said, "It works so much better like this!" We decided to call it the "Ping-Pong Effect." (TMI)

"Shoot High, Aim Low"

jon (1988): In the first line of "Shoot High, Aim Low" is "We hit the blue fields" and he [Trevor] sings "In the blue sedan we couldn't get much further." Now, the blue fields is a part of Nicaragua and as long as you know that, the song makes a lot of sense. I'm the guy in the helicopter going in at ninety miles per hour and I'm going to blow everybody up. A very sick sort of situation. The song is in a way a dedication to live beyond war and at the same time Trevor is singing the dream of love: in the car with a girl having fun. (ST)

alan (1989): "Shoot High, Aim Low" was recorded in the castle [in Caramati, Italy] to achieve a natural reverb sound without using electric reverb. They set up a drum kit in a room where the king used to eat his meals in front of the fire. (WS)

(1995): I came up with the chords. I was playing along with the drum box in the rehearsal room, it was just one of those songs that came out of nowhere. And Trevor walked in—Chris was late for rehearsal—and he said, "Keep playing that." I kept playing it and he started singing this melody over the top and that's where the song came from.

Live it was a great number. We changed the whole ending, we went into a whole series of chord changes. It really built up to the climax. (TMI)

trevor rabin (1995): "Shoot High, Aim Low" is probably my favorite song on the album. (TMI)

"Almost Like Love"

trevor rabin (1995): That song didn't work for me; I didn't like the idea of putting horns on it. It was Chris's baby, but to me horns on a Yes album was like us doing "Sussudio" or something. I saw Yes as being orchestral rather than being *Soul Train*. . . .

I don't think it should have gone on the album. It was this riff that Chris came up with and he was determined that it would go onto the record. It was like Chris was polishing the vase while the building was falling down. He'd say, "But this riff . . ." and I'd say, "Yeah, but Chris, the song around it sucks!" (TMI)

"Love Will Find a Way"

trevor rabin (1991): Stevie Nicks wanted to do it and so I finished it off. And she was really into doing it and she wanted to change some of the lyrics and I said fine. She changed them and was about to do it and when Alan heard it he said, "We've got to do that song." (YGVH)

(1995): I really enjoyed that song, because the lyric "Love will find a way" I thought was a great lyric. I just kept singing it over and over to myself and I was very happy with that song. It's a feel-good song. I put the orchestral piece in the beginning and it was great getting into the studio with the old baton. I felt the song turned out very well; unfortunately, I think a lot of Yes fans listened to it and said, "You're moving too far away from what Yes stands for." (TMI)

"FINAL EYES"

trevor rabin (1995): I enjoyed working on that song from a production and arrangement point of view, because it was a very difficult song to do . . . it goes through so many mood changes. Structurally as a song it didn't completely work and one had to arrange it to work or start again. I think the verse with acoustic guitar and Jon's voice is lovely and I think that song works, but unfortunately it never happened live. (TMI)

"I'M RUNNING"

trevor rabin (1987): We went to SARM Studios, which is Trevor Horn's studio, to do a long and very complex song called "I'm Running." The band was in the studio playing, and even though I'm an engineer, I wasn't thinking about the technical aspect of it. When we went back to listen, I was thinking that any sounds that weren't happening we'd fix later. It turned out that the drum sound was unusable! Alan, to his credit, did the drums again, note for note. There was a lot of salvaging. (GW)

(1995): Chris wrote this riff and he kept playing it to me, to the point where I said, "Oh, come on! Enough already." He kept going "Dunt do dat do . . ." and I said, "All right, all right." I thought, "What can I do with that? Well, maybe a Latin feel might work with it." And so we started messing around with it and playing it in rehearsal and the Latin thing seemed to work. . . . I don't think the song completely works, because some of the vocals that Chris and I did could have been stronger. I'm not one hundred percent happy with it, but I felt the band played well on it. It's a very strange piece of music and maybe that's why I like it. (TMI)

"HOLY LAMB"

jon (1989): Several years ago, I met some spiritual people in Las Vegas, of all places, who had a message for me. They told me about something called the Harmonic Convergence and said that I would be singing songs about it. I woke up the next morning, thinking it had all been a dream and ten years later almost to the day, that event took place. I was singing about the convergence. (CL)

ON JON LEAVING THE BAND IN 1987

jon (1988): I enjoyed working with the guys on the last couple of albums very much. My participation was very strong—it was just one of those things. You feel a turning point in your career . . . I wanted to make something more of an experience in music—a continuum of what I believe really. . . . I wasn't really creating that with Trevor and the guys. (YM)

ANDERSON BRUFORD WAKEMAN HOWE
RELEASED JUNE 1989

Jon Anderson got in touch with Steve Howe, Rick Wakeman, and Bill Bruford about forming a new band. They agreed to the concept and turned over song ideas to Anderson, who fleshed the work out into finished songs. Then they went to Barbados to record the album (with the exception of Steve Howe, who recorded his parts in London) and prepared to tour. During this time things got very sticky between ABWH and Yes. Lawsuits were filed back and forth over who had the rights to the music and the name of Yes. When the dust finally settled it was difficult to say who had really won.

jon (1989): I've always said that I'm waiting for a group to come along and shock me. And I said, "Hey, nothing's happening. I've got to do it myself. I've got to get together with the guys." The first one that I saw was Bill, and he shocked me. His computer drumming is extraordinary. His playing and his attitude were marvelous, and the same with Rick, the same with Steve. He brought some great songs along and it all seemed to fall into place. I decided that it would be a good thing to spend five weeks in an appropriate place like Paris, developing the initial songs, the music. Put it down. Then come to Montserrat, which is an extraordinary beautiful place. There are beautiful people on the island. It was a great album to make here—you feel the energy. (YM)

rick (1989): For some unknown reason this particular combination of musicians is quite frightening. It's weird, because Jon, Bill, Steve, and I only actually played together for two and a half years. But during that period we were four-fifths responsible for *Fragile, Close to the Edge,* and a considerable amount of *Yessongs.* That's pretty terrifying. We were also aware that when Jon, Steve, and I did some things together in the latter years of the seventies, something special was going to come out. So when we started this project, however people might accept it, we knew that this strange chemistry was going to produce something that would excite us. (K)

bill (1995): [on the four-way writing split] It's fair to say that sometimes when music is credited to musicians it is a way of paying them for their general contributions to the music, rather than any specific notes on paper. My name attached to the publishing on that record is symptomatic of a business deal between me and Jon, whereby I was also going to be compensated by some of the publishing. [It was] an attraction to come and play with him. There was a fee, but also a portion of the publishing—that's a quite common arrangement. Actually I didn't have anything whatsoever to do with the writing on that.

I only accepted the project because the music was already pretty much down on tape. It just needed a rhythm section added. So I didn't have to sit in a rehearsal room, dreaming up whether the chord movement should go from F-major to G-major-7. I couldn't go nine rounds in a room with Jon again! He'll win every time. (TMI)

steve (1992): Jon left Yes and joined ABWH partly because of relations with Chris Squire. I'm one of the few lucky people who can write with Jon and get on with him on a personal level. . . . Working with Tony Levin on bass made the *ABWH* album more powerful in a perfectionist way. (GTM)

bill (1994): It was really quite amazing hooking up with Wakeman and Howe and Jon again, who on the whole were the most musical side of it. Squire had gone a bit down the tubes at the time that I met him again in 1990. . . . I was thrilled that he wasn't in ABWH. I thought it was really important that Tony Levin did that, not Chris Squire. (TMI)

steve (1991): ABWH wasn't made of people who were desperate to call themselves Yes. It was more made up of a band, that at least Bill and I felt was a new band and we could not rest totally on the old material. (MTV)

rick (1993): There are bits on the album that are a bit weak. But there are some wonderful strengths in things like "Brother of Mine" and "The Order of the Universe." (TR)

trevor rabin (1995): The *ABWH* album came out at the same time as my solo album. And a guy from Arista said, "We were really kind of worried because 'Something to Hold On To' [from Trevor's album] was number one on Album-Oriented Radio and *ABWH* was number three. It was like a big battle between the two." And I didn't know that—I don't think of music as a battle. I bought the *ABWH* album and just enjoyed it. I didn't listen to it under any other terms. (TMI)

alan (1994): I thought there were a couple of things that were good. I didn't enjoy a lot of it, some of it was weak. (TMI)

chris (1994): I wasn't that impressed. (NFTE)

"THEMES"

bill (1994): There was a moment somewhere around ABWH when it was no longer Jon's thing. He started it and when he came to my house I thought he was inviting me to play on a solo album. So then we get out to Montserrat and he said, "Oh, by the way, Steve Howe's doing this and so is Rick Wakeman." And I said, "Oh, that sounds pretty nice." But you know what happens the minute you put those four in a room; someone's going to say, "Why don't you do concerts and all the rest of it?" So that's how all that happened. But just for a second there, there was a strong drive from Jon. You know . . . "Begone, you everlasting power play machine" or whatever it is. He didn't want to be in the record industry anymore, by God he was going to do what he wanted. Well, that was a little window of opportunity that lasted ten minutes before it slammed shut. (TMI)

"FIST OF FIRE"

steve (1991): I was mixed out of five tracks that I actually put guitar ideas on. I was pretty furious about that. I didn't believe that I had to go there to defend my guitar. I had a real wake-up Dave Gilmour riff on "Fist of Fire," I even put a lute on "The Meeting." So if justice be done, then at another time there will be some remixing going on. (WS)

"BROTHER OF MINE"

jon (1994): This is a song I wrote with Steve Howe for ABWH. It's about a very narrow-minded person that doesn't believe he is part of everybody on this entire planet. We're all one. (CL)

geoff (1994): I thought it was a good collaboration between Steve and myself. I was quite happy that they used it. The whole musical ending section was really written by me, I suppose. (TMI)

steve (1994): It was completely taken from my music and Jon added to it, he could elaborate and stick stuff in. It was a great source of future thinking for me, that Jon and I were exchanging music. It was originally going to be done with Asia and it was called "Lost in America," it was going to be in the film *Lost in America*. This tune really stuck with me, I thought it's a great tune; it's a hit chorus, but not the words. So I changed the words and called it "(Have You) Forgotten Love." I changed the verses, which were written by John [Wetton], and Geoff, and Geoff wrote the chorus structure. I wrote a whole set of lyrics for it.

Around the time of GTR I wrote a song about where my brother was in Australia, because I hadn't seen him for so long; it was called "Long Lost Brother of Mine." I wanted a chorus; I had the verses, which became "Brother of Mine" as you know it. So you could say "Brother of Mine" was written by me, I wrote the words "brother of mine," I wrote all of the structure, except the introduction structure, which Jon wrote. It was terrific construction, Jon did an excellent job. There's another song involved as well called "Full Moon," and I told Jon, "Please expand this." And he stuck that in with "Brother of Mine." You know, "Nothing can come between us." It was probably the most underclarified [song] in how much I'd done. (TMI)

"BIRTHRIGHT"

jon (1989): I read a book called *Song Line*. It's about the Aborigine magic, the knowledge of the Earth Mother, the way the Aborigine life revolves around the Earth Mother and how this relates to the American Indian, the Eskimos, and the Aborigine people of the world. The song is really about a sad moment in history in 1954 when the British government set off an atom bomb which had an effect that reached all the tribes. While I was in America I was told that the Americans were testing the atom bomb around the same time and a lot of Apache Indians were killed. So, in relative terms, this is a song about an accident that happened. We have to remember them, learn about them, and learn from that mistake. We have to regard people as human beings, regardless of their color or creed. (CL)

bill (1994): There was a moment there where ABWH could have become a good group. That was just a moment somewhere around the tune "Birthright." And we would be playing that thing nightly and there's a bit in the middle where it's kind of ascending and Rick is doing this sort of Elgar business on the keyboards and it was genuinely a tremendously exciting moment before it comes into some sort of Aboriginal drumming. Steve has a very light acoustic guitar sound on top of this huge keyboard. And this was tremendous doing this every night and I'm thinking that somewhere around here there is a genuine future for these people, but I think too quickly the band was snubbed off in its prime, because we weren't allowed to go on being ABWH. There was all kinds of legal problems and it had to turn into Yes, [and] it didn't have to at all, of course. (TMI)

"The Meeting"

rick (1989): I had just sat down at the piano and started playing away, as musicians are wont to do in the studio while everyone is mucking around in the control room. Jon came out and said, "What key are you doing that in?" I told him C, I think. Then he said, "I've got a song. I've had it in my brain for such a long time, but I haven't heard the right thing to go with it. Let me sing it for you." So we worked literally for ten minutes to put them together, then went back to what we were doing. The following day around nine o'clock at night, Jon and I finished a meal together, then went down into the studio, ran the tape, and did two versions of "The Meeting" . . . It was a very pleasant move away from the way the rest of the album was put together. (K)

jon (1990): When we played in Germany, the Wall had come down earlier that week, and I dedicated the song to the East Germans and the West Germans. When you're coming together after so many years . . . well, this is a song about coming together. It's called "The Meeting." There were people just crying. And you could understand. Relatives from the East were just flooding the West. They're doing it every day now, with freedom. (CL)

"Quartet"

steve (1989): [Part I: I Wanna Learn] That, to me, is very much home-spun in feel. I don't just stop at doing the guitar, I like to color it and use the guitar family, which you can tell on this piece. (G)

"Teakbois"

steve (1993): I did provide quite a large chunk of ABWH music and some ideas. Jon went off with them and I allowed him the freedom and the trust to arrange some of his music in with it. And Jon used ideas in sometimes intriguing ways. And other times—we didn't know what "Teakbois" was all about from the minute it started to the minute it ended. (YM)

"The Order of the Universe"

steve (1992): I was actually writing a song about the American Indian around 1982. I was trying to get it for the second Asia album, called *Alpha*. Basically, the song was supposed to be about the Indians belonging on their land, and that this was part of the order of things. But then, something was coming that was terribly wrong, the white people's invasion. But I needed a canon idea, where something had to repeat, and I found myself humming "order of the universe." It was just spontaneous, as I was monkeying about with the vocals at the microphone. So I put it in the song, and the other guys in Asia liked the sound, the hypnotic-ness of it. They said, "The order of what? . . . the order of the universe?" They thought that sounded quite nice. I felt that I actually should have made more of it. But the song didn't make it on the album. . . . So, I met up with Jon Anderson years later, 1988 I guess, and he says, "What songs have you written?" So I played two or three songs that I'd written currently [including "Birthright" and "Brother of Mine"], and pulled out "Barren Land" from years before. And he liked the order of the universe thing, as one of many bits. After that, Jon went to Paris, and I met with him there later. I heard some of the tapes he had been putting together, and he said he wanted that order of the universe sound for a particular song. And we ended up having this new song, now called "The Order of the Universe." It became the song title, with a whole different story or meaning with it. . . . It felt particularly good doing "Order of the Universe" on stage, prompting people to think, "Well, is there an order?" (MT)

"LET'S PRETEND"

UNION
RELEASED APRIL 1991

When ABWH went to record their second album, they ran into some difficulties: the first being their producer, Jonathan Elias, who apparently didn't have a clue as to what made the band tick; the second being a huge backlog of weak material that just wasn't working out. Jon Anderson placed a call to Trevor Rabin seeking suitable songs for the record, and the idea for the union of the two feuding groups was discussed and later realized. It's a shame that *Union* doesn't reflect the powerful talent that existed in this supergroup, but the weak material and horrible production choices doomed it from the start. The Around the World in Eighty Dates tour was a much more enjoyable and successful venture.

rick (1992): I call it the Onion album, because every time I hear it, it brings tears to my eyes. (TR)

trevor rabin (1995): I think everyone will say that *Union* is a black mark on the band. I know a lot of Yes fans don't like *Big Generator* and there is some low moments on the album. But there are also, in my opinion, some of the best stuff that I've been involved with Yes on that. While *Union* has some good stuff, it was why it was done and how it was done from a nineteenth-floor decision kind of thing [that upset me] . . . and I think to myself that I should have fought it a bit. (TMI)

(1994): Jon called me during that *ABWH* album, the second one, and he said the album was going really well and stuff, but they were looking for one more song. What I read into that was they needed a single. Basically I got three songs that I thought might be appropriate that I wasn't going to use, and sent them to the record company. What I said in the letter was, "Choose one of these songs, if you so desire; otherwise, please send the tape back." To cut a long story short, they chose all of the songs and that led to them saying, "Why don't we put this whole comprehensive reunion thing together?" Basically the suits got involved, thinking, "Boy, we could make a lot of money here." And so, even though they thought they were manipulating the band, it was something that was useful and convenient to everyone, because we wanted to go on the road, and it was a quick way . . . there were demos that I put on that album. Jon came in and sang on top of these demos, and we just stuck them on the album. So half of it was an ABWH album, and the other half was a Yes album. (K)

steve (1994): Bill and I were particularly surprised that we were going to change midstream and become Yes. We had this group ABWH, which was on the up and up, and Yes were kind of—well, we didn't know where they were. In a way, Bill and I were surprised anybody lost faith in us at that point, but in comparison, releasing a record called Yes had more potential exposure. It was commercial thinking, which once again doesn't help a group like us. (GTRSP)

rick (1991): Jon has always believed that we would be able to get together and play. He really has always believed it. He might not say it publicly, but he always has. (MTV)

steve (1991): *Union* does represent in a strangely uncanny way the only way this Yes incarnation could come together. It was a difficult project from the outset, which was more in control of the producers than the players and that required a lot of compromise from everybody. It may be a bit uncomfortable in spots, but that's part of the creative process that went into it. (GS)

chris (1993): Just about everyone in the world played on the ABWH tracks. Half the time it wasn't Rick when it was supposed to be Rick. The same thing happened with Steve: it was other people. Jimmy [Haun, guitarist for the Chris Squire Experiment] played a lot of guitar Steve thought was him! He didn't realize until about halfway through the European leg of the tour that it was somebody else playing on the album. He hadn't even listened to it. I told him he might want to check it out and he got very annoyed. I don't quite know how that happened—whether Jon was in control of it with the producer, I don't know. It's definitely a very strange album. (WS)
    (1994): I think it's important to note that on the album there was no point where the eight of us were playing together on any one song. It was really like Jon was going back and forth between the ABWH band and us like a loose cannon. (VG)

steve (1994): I don't think *Union* was a success. I think my track "Masquerade" was because it cost nothing to make—I did it at my home away from all the arguments and politics—and it got a Grammy nomination, which was pure justice to me. People spent $2 million making music that no one took notice of and I cut "Masquerade" in fifteen minutes at home on a two-channel Revox deck and lots of people liked it. And looking back I think we should have carried on with Anderson, Bruford, Wakeman, and Howe and not gotten back together with Yes. (GTRSP)

rick (1991): When we were told that we could all get together legally and play, Arista wanted the album finished hastily. The problem was that Steve Howe and I had a lot of other heavy commitments, so a lot of our stuff was stuck in the computer and had not been transferred to digital tape. That, sadly, gave the producer a lot more carte blanche than he should ever have had in editing what I'd done, even to the extent of changing what I had played, because it was so easy: You just sit there, play with the little mouse, and things can come and go. The thing that annoyed me more than anything was that even if you're unavailable to come in and do things, there are such things as telephones for consultation on the pieces of music you're involved in. To be honest, it took me a long time to play *Union* all the way through. The first cassette I received from Arista went out of the limo window after about fifteen minutes. The next one went out of a hotel window. It's taken me a long time to calm down and be rational about it. In a nutshell, I am one hundred percent unhappy with every piece of keyboard work that's on that album. There is not one piece on there I can put my hand on and say to anybody who knows me as a player, "Listen to this." (K)

(1993): What happened was the amalgamation came through during my first Classical Connection tour. I got a fax saying we were called Yes and I thought, "Oh, that's nice, that's good. I'm very proud to be in Yes." Then they said they were putting two albums together and I asked whether I could play on the other songs. They said yes, but it had to be done next week. And I was in the middle of a tour! So the next thing is I get hold of this album, and most of California are on it. There are more people on it than came to the first show. (TR)

alan (1994): I have mixed emotions about *Union*. . . . It's not my favorite album, there are some things that could have been done a lot better if we'd kind of sat down and did it in the old way where we'd revamped some of it. But it wasn't to be because of time. (TMI)

bill (1994): The only [album of my work] I actively hate is the Yes *Union* record. I thought that was a terrible record. Absolutely awful, an embarrassing record. It cost way too much money. There was no direction at all. It was just a record company thing where they were screwing the band rotten. All egos colliding. It was the most awful album to make. (S)

The lasting problem with all members of Yes is that they tend to listen to the manager and record company too much. They have long ago given up their rights, their self-determination, which is a great shame.

In the early days of the band we did what we wanted, but eventually too much money was consumed and the thing lost its way and I'm glad that I'm no longer part of it. (TMI)

"I WOULD HAVE WAITED FOREVER"

steve (1991): This song very much has the Anderson-Howe look about it. There's a lot of structure from me, a more ethereal "Brother of Mine" feel, if you like, in which it keeps making transitions. The track is very Howe and the lyrics are very Anderson. (GW)

"Shock to the System"

steve (1991): "Shock to the System" is one that has more of rocky and riffy Telecaster sound; it really grooves. I think we were looking to balance the arty side of the group with a more primal force. (GW)

jonathan elias (1991): It came from a riff on a tail-out of a song that Steve played for me. I immediately jumped on it and said, "Let's do something with this." Jon, Steve, and I then wrote a chorus for it one afternoon after lunch in Le Val. (K)

"Masquerade"

steve (1994): When I did "Masquerade" for Arista Records, I also did "Baby Georgia" and a small collection of solos for them on Spanish guitar. The songs were sent to New York and they chose "Masquerade." The funny thing is that I was almost not going to send them that track, since I really didn't think it was as strong as the other three. I've always found the hardest thing to do was to record solo guitar and make it sound masterful. (GTRSP)

"Lift Me Up"

chris (1991): [Trevor and I] had a dictionary on the left and we were just having fun with the song. And we were doing things like opening up the dictionary and pointing a finger on a word and that's how we came up with "imperial." (UP)

trevor rabin (1991): Lyrically the verse was a little dark, we tried to make it somewhat vague as to what it was about, but one of the pictures is that it's a homeless person . . . "Look around, I've got nowhere to stay . . . you look me up, you look me down" the guy who goes into the restaurant to use the bathroom and they look at him, "No, you can't come in here." And he just looks to the sky [and says], "Lift me up and turn me over," you know, help me out. (UP)

(1995): "Lift Me Up" makes me cringe, because I think the mix is dreadful. What happened was I did two mixes and Clive Davis didn't like them. So Chris said, "Why don't you just get someone else to mix it?" And I said, "That's a very good idea." We got Paul Fox, who is actually very good at his job, it's just that no one gave him any idea of what was wanted. The original mix was so much better than what ended up on the album. (TMI)

"Without Hope (You Cannot Start the Day)"

steve (1991): We're not so keen on too many love songs—that's not very much like us. (GW)

jonathan elias (1991): I recorded the original scratch track one afternoon at Jon's house. Then we sent the tape to Rick to have him do the real part, and what we got back sounded like a Rachmaninoff piano concerto. It's great that Rick can play like that, but Jon and I really wanted something simple and gentle. We ended up doing it ourselves in my studio late the night before mixing, on an old acoustic piano with the mikes in the middle of the room to get that feeling of it being late at night in a faraway land. (K)

"SAVING MY HEART"

trevor rabin (1991): It's similar to "Owner of a Lonely Heart" in that I didn't think it was appropriate for a Yes album. It's kind of a pop reggae tune, if you like, with a bluesy guitar solo. Jon and I were working on "Lift Me Up" when I first played the track for him, which I was originally going to do with Roger Hodgson [of Supertramp]. Jon loved it, said he wanted to do it, and so we did. (GW)

(1995): Although I thought the song had potential, the way it came out makes me cringe a little. That was really just a very basic demo and when I hear it, it sounds so demo-ey to me. What we did is we took the demo and tried to fix it. It just didn't turn out the way I wanted it to. (TMI)

"MIRACLE OF LIFE"

trevor rabin (1991): It's kind of a protest song. . . . I was watching CNN's world report and there was a thing on Denmark with what's happening with the dolphins, how they're being slaughtered. It just kind of got to me, and so the verses to the song are a little dark. (UP)

tony (1919): We thought it would be a departure from *Big Generator* or *90125*. Trevor wrote it and it seemed so Yessy. (K)

steve (1993): I think "Miracle of Life" is very good. (NFTE)

"SILENT TALKING"

steve (1991): There was another song that was segued with "Silent Talking," a song I wrote called "Seven Castles." "Seven Castles" was some of the best guitar work I did on the whole album, but on the finished version it was cut off as Jon came in to sing. I'm playing and then I suddenly hear Jon's singing, and I said, "Hang on, you know, I need this space." And I was desperately hoping he was going to stop singing because I really captured something there. Of course, you don't get that feeling there because Jon's got his hook going and my guitar's floating around the back. (WS)

"THE MORE WE LIVE—LET GO"

chris (1995): It wasn't written particularly about any personal incident. We just sat down and wrote the song. I wrote all the music to start with and Billy [Sherwood] did a lot of the tune and quite a lot of the lyrics too. (TMI)

alan (1994): I've got demos of Billy singing the song in its original form and it's really good. He's been a Yes fan for many years and he knew us so well that he was almost a part of the band. (TMI)

chris (1995): In many ways I prefer Billy's vocal performance of it. There's a different style of singing; Billy's is much more laid back than Jon's. I happen to think it suits the song very well. But there again Jon interprets it in his own way and it's like that often happens. Bob Dylan would write a song and someone else would have a hit with it and maybe he wouldn't, but later you preferred the way Dylan sang the song. (TMI)

"ANGKOR WAT"

jonathan elias (1991): This song was actually done on one of the last days I had Rick. I wanted to get something with him playing keyboards, just doing an atmospheric thing. We did all these different layers of keyboards; he never heard the other layers, he would just overdub without hearing them. (MN)

"DANGEROUS"
"HOLDING ON"

jonathan elias (1991): "Holding On" never really became the track that we had hoped it would be. We always had more hope in the song than was realized. (MN)

"EVENSONG"

bill (1995): It was me and Tony [Levin], we put that song together. It was very loose. We had a duet on the ABWH tour and that was the middle section of the duet. He played something and I played something immediately and we called it "Evensong" and split the publishing. It didn't take long to do. "Evensong" is the Anglican evening prayers in the Church of England. It is a church tone. Madmatins is what you sing in the morning and Evensong is in the evening. It is the reflective time of day, it's lovely actually. At six in the evening everyone goes in and it's often a very simple service, maybe half an hour. (TMI)

"TAKE THE WATER TO THE MOUNTAIN"

jon (1991): It's a simple song, really. Take the water back to the mountains and give the mountains the energy they need. It's a reference to our ancient knowledge. About halfway through the track, the music becomes very ancient-sounding and very rhythmic. (GW)

TALK
RELEASED MARCH 1994

The idea for the *Union* lineup to record a communal album never got off of the ground. Phil Carson of Victory Records wanted the *90125* lineup to make a record for his label, so Steve Howe, Bill Bruford, and Rick Wakeman did not appear on *Talk*. Trevor Rabin oversaw the production of this album and decided to record the whole thing on computer. This made for a frustrating

Trevor with his self-customized
Fender Stratocaster.

Tony Kaye accompanies Trevor Rabin on a solo spot.

Yes at the Harley Davidson Cafe.
KAREN HEARN/COURTESY MUSIC NEWS NETWORK

eighteen-month project for him, but the resulting sonic clarity was well worth it. *Talk* features excellent songwriting, performances, and production and is easily the best record the band has done since *90125*.

steve (1993): Bill and I aren't working with them due to the lack of insight they have. So I think Phil Carson had been very silly as well to take on Yes without two key members in it. [This was before Rick Wakeman dropped out of the project as well.]

I think we had something in *Union* that was difficult to perpetuate. It wasn't impossible, we had to wake up and share. . . . Yes means sharing. The group is about hours in rehearsal rooms cooking up how to turn three chords into a masterpiece! We all played a role in that. (MNN)

trevor rabin (1994): Phil Carson from Victory Music called me and said, "Look, I want to do a Yes album, and I want you to produce it. I want Jon to sing on it, basically I want the *90125* lineup, and because of your relationship with Rick it would be nice if he was involved." However, there were certain things with Rick's manager that got in the way. . . .

[On] *Big Generator,* and consequently other stuff, I could feel the frustration in Jon that, although he was involved, it was basically me writing the songs and Jon trying to work on top of them. So when this project came up, I thought, "Well, if I'm going to be the producer, then I really need to look at how the thing's going to be done in the best possible way." So I realized, the best possible way is, if Jon's the singer, then I need to work real closely with him to provide him with the best possible platform to sing on. And you know, Jon singing his lyrics, he feels much more comfortable with it. So I wrote a lot of stuff and went over. He was staying at a motel in San Clemente, and I rented a room there for a week or two. We just sat there and banged all the stuff out [on] an acoustic guitar and two ghetto blasters, one to play my demos from and another one to record the live vocals on. It was real high-tech! Bottom-line, that's how we did it. So rather than get Jon involved in at the last possible minute, I got him involved. The two of us really worked hard as a team on it, which led to it being a better album for us. (K)

tony (1994): Trevor's really come into his own with this album. There were a lot of detours and little directions for him to find his place in Yes. It's weird—the poor guy has been in the band for twelve years and just now started writing with Jon. I think he's done a fantastic job. I know how much time, effort, and dedication he's put into it. It's not easy. (WS)

jon (1994): It's a special album. A couple of months ago I was thinking, "How far does Yes go?" Obviously to me and a lot of people around the world, this album has really touched a nerve. The more I hear the album, the more I appreciate Trevor's work. (YV)

chris (1994): We had been working on ideas for a couple of years, so as soon as we signed the deal with Victory we were ready to go. This record is different because it's the first time Trevor—who was also the producer—wrote together with Jon from the outset. When we did *90125* and *Big Gen-*

erator, Jon came in very late and added only a few bits to what we had. For this record I stepped aside in those areas to allow that union to happen; I have only a couple of writing credits, but I'm very happy with what Trevor and Jon came up with. (BP)

alan (1994): I thought *Talk* was a *90125* of the nineties. And if it had been handled as well as it was by the band in the studio by the companies around it . . . it would have done the same as *90125.* Also the climate made a difference, in what the album was up against. But I'm certainly proud of it, I think it's one of the best things the band has ever done. It seems Victory wasn't able to promote it the way it should have been, they didn't have it quite together. Trevor did a fantastic job on it. (TMI)

trevor rabin (1995): The record company thought the album was going to sell five million copies. They had very overbloated expectations. It didn't do as well as we'd like it to have done, but we're still happy with it. The whole radio programming of the kind of music that Yes is was changing as the album was being made. Right now you can look back and say, "We shouldn't have gone that route—we should have tried to promote the album without even bothering with radio." Even though "The Calling" was number one on Album-Oriented Radio, that format is dead. . . . There just wasn't a platform for the record that Victory knew about. (TMI)

steve (1994): Well, of course I've heard it. I wonder if any of them listened as closely to *The Grand Scheme of Things* as I did to *Talk.* I listened to it and I found that it was very uncharacteristic to me. The approach wasn't very Yessish. In most respects it's a good record, except to the point of being a Yes record. It doesn't seem to be a Yes record. (YV)

trevor rabin (1995): I've read what Steve has had to say about *Talk* and I find it very presumptuous of him to make these comments. He has a different way of listening to things as opposed to the people who might have enjoyed the album. Very often when I feel we have achieved something good, like *90125*—Steve doesn't say it isn't good, he'll say it isn't Yessish. The original design and flavor of Yes was not me, it was Steve more so than Peter Banks. I'm one of the first to acknowledge that Steve's writing was an important aspect of what Yes used to do. But after being with the band for thirteen years I feel Yes became something else, not just because of me, but the whole character of it had changed. I don't think that [what he said] is only a slight on me, I think it's a slight on everyone. It sounds like he's saying, "Without me there can't be anything that remotely resembles Yes." So I don't feel it is appropriate to say that it's not Yessish, but by all means say, "It doesn't sound like the Yes I used to play in." (TMI)

"THE CALLING"

trevor rabin (1994): "The Calling" musically was written around the guitar riff and it all kind of evolved and revolves around that. Once Jon and I started getting into it lyrically the feeling was just to do not so much a preaching thing, but just calling out for everyone to get together. (MNN)

jon (1994): Basically, we're living in a "local history." What I mean by that is that we're only living [with the benefit of] a three-thousand-year history [the history of mankind]. So we don't know what went on ten thousand or twenty thousand years ago on this planet. We're holding the right to rearrange things because the time we get into the twenty-first century we will learn a lot more about our real destiny and origins. (TMP)

We were all in school choirs and we just sing what we want to sing and it seems to blend naturally. This album is very strong with Trevor and Chris arranging a lot of the vocal harmonies. We all have different-sounding voices so it sounds very powerful. (TPRS)

chris (1994): "The Calling" is fun to play live; it's a good example of separate vocal and bass lines going at the same time, which leads to some tricky spots. (BP)

"I'M WAITING"

trevor rabin (1994): I had an idea and I started writing this idea and it was "I'm Waiting," and it was so easy. It just kind of came out. I didn't have to think too much and the song came out and it took me a day from beginning to end. I played it for Jon and it really got him motivated. He loved it. He wrote most of the lyrics right there and then and sang the final vocal right there and then. Most of the vocal on that track was done that day, almost immediately. It was totally spontaneous. (MNN)

jon (1994): It's great when that happens . . . it's real pure music, because you're not thinking about it. This is definitely one of my favorite songs. (TPRS)

tony (1994): This is a great song for Jon to sing—a delicate balance of heavy and light styles. (WS)

"REAL LOVE"

trevor rabin (1994): I had just finished a book recently, *A Brief History of Time* by Stephen Hawking. In "Real Love" the lyric goes "Far away in the depths of Hawking's mind/To the animal, the primalistic grind /You bring me reason, the simple fact of life . . ." the love thing, you know: that whether you're as far ahead as a guy like Hawking is, or as primitive as an ape, you still have emotions. That was kind of inspired because I think I had a crash [on the computer]. I thought, "Oh, damn." And I was having a mental block on what lyrics to put there. Jon had written some lyrics in the chorus and called this "Real Love" I thought, "I've got to put this bridge in there and I want it to relate and have that contrasting thing from this extreme to that extreme. How am I going to get that across?" So I came out and I was finishing off the Hawking book . . . and I thought, "There it is!"(G)

jon (1994): The fire that's burning is the fire of confusion within our souls because we're watching CNN all the time thinking, "that's the real world." That's not the real world, it's a beautiful world out there. I mean, nothing happens around Binghamton. One or two people get busted up, and there's maybe one murder a year, you never know. You're surrounded by beauty and nature and a community that just gets on with life. But the energy of intellect is saying, "What's happening, what's going on, where's the war?" We forget that we're surrounded by so much wonderful energy. (TMP)

Real love isn't physical. It's a spiritual entity. To activate the spiritual entity is to be on the mission. To believe in being. (YV)

tony (1994): "Real Love" is mainly Chris's song. It's pretty heavy, to say the least. (WS)

chris (1994): There's proof of the evolution of my style: I wrote most of the music of that tune, including the really basic bass part. It fits the song— but if someone else had asked me to play that line I probably would have refused! (BP)

"STATE OF PLAY"

trevor rabin (1994): That originated from I was driving somewhere and a police car or an ambulance passed me by with a siren going and I thought, "Wow! That's a great sound!" And it overtook me and I thought that's an amazing sound with the Doppler effect and everything as it goes by. That gave me the idea for the screeching kind of guitar sound in the beginning. (MNN)

jon (1994): The children of the world are really now the ones that can split the atom correctly. The people who have been screwing around with the atom . . . over the last fifty years have done nothing but harm. They haven't created anything useful. (TMP)

chris (1994): "State of Play" was a conscious effort to combine that type of [hip-hop] groove with heavy rock guitars, and that's what we came up with. (BP)

"WALLS"

trevor rabin (1994): I actually wrote it quite a long time ago. It was not an afterthought, but it was, I mean it was always in the back of my head that maybe we should check it out. It was the last thing we did on the album and I wasn't quite sure if we were going to do it or not. I spoke with Roger [Hodgson] and my concern was I had a version that I'd done with Roger which was really good. I was kind of happy with it and I was concerned not so much if the Yes version would lose something or gain something, but more whether it would fit in with the rest of the tracks, which were already done and I felt pretty cohesive in how they knitted together. But once it was done it really worked for me. (MNN)

"WHERE WILL YOU BE"

trevor rabin (1994): There was an Australian movie which they asked me to do the signature tune for and that was going to be the signature tune for this movie. I played it for Jon and he liked it. He said, "Look, I don't want to touch anything on it. I just want to write a lyric to this melody." I think it's one of the best lyrics on the album. (MNN)

chris (1994): "Where Will You Be" is sort of our version of a folk song. (BP)

"ENDLESS DREAM"

jon (1994): I think it's exactly as good as anything we've done. The last third is a remarkable musical structure. I'm in heaven when I'm singing that like I am when I do "Close to the Edge" or "Awaken." It really works on a par with them. It's very modern, very hectic at the beginning, very wild. It's very exciting music, and I have a feeling that on stage it's really going to take off. (TMP)

The idea [of doing long pieces] is very, very simple. We are so used to fast food, fast energy, fast flicks, fast videos, fast songs . . . isn't it good sometimes to sit back and get involved with something that is very true to our heart and soul? Life is an incredible event and we should sit back and take it easy and really enjoy it. Sometimes to hear a long piece of music can take you on a beautiful journey and that's what we've always dreamed of doing. Throughout the career of Yes that's what we've done: long pieces of music to take people on a journey. . . . On this album there is a piece that will take you on the real ultimate journey. (TPRS)

trevor rabin (1995): The middle section with the dreamy keyboard part was part of an orchestral piece called "October" that I'd written for full orchestra. I used the middle section and made it more synthetic than orchestral with synthesizers. So that part was already in existence. The beginning piano part was something I'd written for a movie score and it was much longer. But I decided not to give it to this guy for the movie and I kept it for this song. I had the chords for the bridge section which I played to Jon and he loved that part so we kept messing around with it. He ended up writing "So take your time . . ." the lyrics that ended up over it. I had the chorus that went with that bridge "It's the last time . . ." What was exciting was how the song modulated to a minor third and the sustained note goes from a fifth to a third in the new key. I kept doing that and the modulations just seemed to work so nicely.

It was one of those things where the computer was invaluable, when I was trying to piece it all together. What I was able to do was chop the song and move the sections around. It was a very time-consuming song—not to write, but to piece together. The guitar solo at the end was going to be much longer, kind of like "Starship Trooper" where it keeps going around and around, but then we had this great quiet part to end on and so I chopped the guitar solo down. (TMI)

chris (1994): That's sort of Trevor's version of Yes from the *Close to the Edge* years—it's a classic example of us ripping ourselves off! The lick is in $^{15}/_8$, so it took us a while, but we got it together. (BP)

In May 1995 Yes went through another series of personnel changes. Trevor Rabin and Tony Kaye both decided to leave the band, allowing the door to be open for Steve Howe and Rick Wakeman to rejoin Yes. This marks the first time since 1979 that this particular lineup has been in existence and the future promise of a new album and tour is very exciting for any Yes fan.

ON TREVOR RABIN LEAVING

trevor rabin (1995): I actually tried to leave two months earlier, but Chris had talked me out of it. I was having arguments with Jon and that's why I was leaving. Chris came around to my house and said, "You can't leave! What have you got on the go that's inspiring you to do this?" I said, "It's not about what I want to do or what I have to do—it's about what I don't want to do any longer. There are things that I find burdening and they are pulling at me." So I spoke to Chris and he talked me out of leaving, so I called Jon and said, "I'm going to stick it out a little longer, but we've got to talk things out." Anyway, the decision was something that had been building up in me for a long time. It was just a gut feeling that it was time for me to move on; the projects that I've been working on are very different than Yes music. After a lengthy discussion with my wife the night before I left, I just decided after thirteen years with the band and after completing an album I was very proud of, that I was leaving on a high note. One of my regrets was that Rick and I were not going to work together in Yes, but we are talking about doing something together in the future. I've enjoyed my time with the band and there are no hard feelings between us. (TMI)

ON THE ROAD

"ANOTHER TOWN

AND ONE

MORE SHOW"

As Alan White once said, "Playing live is what this band is all about!" I couldn't agree with him more, because seeing Yes perform is not just a concert experience, but a musical event like no other. In addition to the intense and intricate music being played, Yes would make the show a visual treat as well. They pioneered the use of elaborate stage setups (courtesy of Roger Dean, Martin Dean, and Michael Tait), costumes, lighting, lasers, and so on to create otherworldly effects.

ON PLAYING ONSTAGE

steve (1991): Touring is a funny kind of life. It's a peculiar working holiday from real life; one that revolves around six strings and two pickups. (GS)

bill (1982): A gig itself, a live performance is really the cream; it's the tip of the iceberg. It's all the work underneath that's important. When you're playing a live performance you're more or less presenting prepared material. There might be some improvising, there might not, in different ratios. You're presenting something fairly prepared, even if it's just the twelve years worth of work you've put into music up until that moment. And so I think the gig is fun. I think it should be fun . . . you must enjoy playing and not worry too much about it, at that stage whether you're a good drummer or bad drummer or anything else like that. You must be at ease with yourself and realize that this now is as good as a musician as you are. There's no point in getting nervous, simply relax and enjoy playing. And I think that enjoyment will communicate to an audience. I don't think you have to ham it up, over-act, or pose for an audience in any way. I think they can see very clearly whether you're feigning or acting. Simple enjoyment of the music is far and away the best remedy for all colds. (BB)

steve (1977): I'm very cool-headed about playing live, but once I'm up there, I do feel it a lot. I'm always feeding off of it; I want to do it right. I have this feeling that if I play a wrong note, I've got to make up for it a few bars later, until I'm feeling good again. I can sometimes sense the excitement of the gig affecting the other people in the band as much as it's affecting me. Then all my concentration goes into pulling it in the direction I think it should go. (GP)

(1976): I've always felt that the stage is the place where you've got to be tremendously honest. But other people don't see that at all; they see it as a place where they can be somebody else. I think both ideas are admirable, it just depends how good you are at whichever one you choose. I have always thrown myself really wide open on stage and sometimes that'll show if something goes wrong and I don't know what I'm supposed to do. (BRG)

patrick (1991): I like dancing on stage. I like the movement of the body going from one keyboard to another. Sometimes a certain movement helps to translate some ideas into music, and that is affected by how your keyboards are displayed. I like that element of risk. When I had those twenty-four keyboards with Yes, I was jumping around like a trapeze artist on stage, or maybe more like a monkey. (K)

steve (1991): I realized over twenty years ago when I first went on stage in North America that a guitarist needs to focus the audience on himself, and understand that by displaying some sense of movement, the movement itself can draw the audience closer to the music. Even if nobody likes what I'm doing prancing about, I'd still do it. (GS)

peter (1994): Playing live was always good [with Yes]. I have great memories about that. Any personal differences we had among the band quickly dissolved when we were on stage. And when it was a good night it was a really good night. (YV)

jon (1989): Eye contact is half the game on stage, you know? You just look at each other and know that this is the right time to hit the beat a bit louder than usual or a bit softer than usual. (ABWH)

Jon swings a baseball bat almost as well as he performs "I've Seen All Good Peop

alan (1985): I just know that every time I get behind my drums the audience will make me rise to the occasion, no matter how I'm feeling backstage or back at the hotel room. (R)

steve (1977): There are things that I'll play at home and think, "Well, that's got to be on my album! Everybody'll go crazy over it." Of course, it doesn't always work out that way. But on the other hand, playing in front of an audience can take you up the same road. You can surprise yourself— play things that you almost thought you couldn't play. Somebody mentioned in a review that I never play the same solo in "Close to the Edge" twice. In quite a few ways, it is always different and that has a great deal to do with the audience. A lot of my technical striving, my improvisation, comes from them. (GP)

bill (1994): We didn't bother with accurate tempo necessarily. Things could speed up at the end of this or they could slow down at the beginning of that, a bit like an orchestra would breathe, you know? Because that was all before click tracks. Linking music to movies and the demands of advertisers and all the rest of it. We thought we were a symphony orchestra so when we wanted to we'd speed up a bit and when we wanted to we'd slow down a bit. (TMI)

steve (1976): On stage, I'll often get the feeling on certain nights that I'll attempt not to play the same lick as last night. Even with the type of music we play, there are some nights when you can pull if off. You'll be looking around at everyone else in the group, and they'll be thinking, "Are you going to play something different? Because if you do, I think I'll be able to keep it together," and everybody's keeping it together for each other so that we can jump off the deep end at certain times. (BRG)

eddie (1992): At some point after the *Fragile* album, they talked me into coming on the road with them and doing live sound and making them sound like they did on record—even better, hopefully. I had two tape machines so that I could just cue in—although it wasn't a Milli Vanilli–type thing—certain overdubs that they couldn't accomplish all at the same time. Maybe a church organ here or a vocal part there to add a touch of the record. (M)

chris (1976): Yes hasn't gone down badly since I can remember. At a concert, the first thirty rows are always full of the most enthusiastic fans; it's very difficult to judge how you're doing. When you're a major group, there's always a lot of people who're going to love you whatever you do. (C)
(1992): I enjoy performing. I don't particularly enjoy traveling. But being in different places, playing to different audiences, yes, I enjoy it. When the show is over, the rest of the day sucks, really. (YM)

alan (1994): I thought on this tour [for *Talk*] the band was the tightest it's ever been. And I think that's due to the fact that we did a lot of preparation and rehearsal for this tour. I started doing rehearsals in the beginning of February and the first gig was in June! (TMI)

steve (1976): When we're on stage doing a selection from our recorded work, I occasionally don't get off on it. When that happens, you'll find me playing in the dressing room after the gig. I won't just finish a set and say "Well, that's okay," because when I feel like that, I've got to play something. I might just plug in my Telecaster, turn up the amp, and go crazy for ten minutes playing very elementary guitar. Because of the complexities of performing a big number where this has to be right, you get to the point where you'd just like to play anything. That's why we get into encores. We can play and not feel paranoid or inhibited. It's not really performing. It's more like we're playing in a club and letting off steam. (BRG)

chris (1976): JFK was the biggest gig the band has ever done [until 1985, when they played to 400,000 at the Rock in Rio show]. There was about 110,000 people in JFK. It was a fantastic place to play, it really was. It's so beautifully laid out, and it was really one of the best sounds that I've experienced in an open-air gig. You just have to be adjusted to doing it, really. We had a PA that was equivalent to fourteen ordinary systems and it was on three levels on each side of the stage. It was really lovely. (C)

steve (1994): The main thing is the separation from the people you raised, your kids, and the people that you love, like your wife. But that's part of your life, it's not something that happened suddenly once. It's been going on all the time, so it's fundamental. It's just a very big sacrifice; they make it and I make it. Sometimes you wonder why the hell you do do it. We're driven and I've got a sense of desire to do this. It must mean something, so I keep doing it. (TMI)

On Seeing the Band Play Live

trevor horn (1980): I remember when they played the fourth side of *Topographic Oceans,* they got to the end and Jon sang that bit, "And I will be there." I remember thinking I'd love to be there too! . . . or I am there. To me it was the perfect concert because it had the power. It had the strength of really heavy rock, but there was also the musicality—the lightness and melody too and the variation. It didn't pound my ears into submission the way other rock concerts I'd seen had done . . . and bore the ass off me in a half hour. It kind of took me all over the place. (R)

tony (1985): The thing I liked best about Yes after I left was the way they played live. I really liked them live. I saw them on several occasions and really enjoyed them. It was always a very professional show. (R)

peter (1991): I think the best band they had was the *90125* thing. I saw them play at Wembley and I thought it was very, very good indeed. (YHS)

On the Union Tour

steve (1991): Sometimes I can feel the energy that I'm generating build up, and it's as if eight people are sitting together and joining hands.

Chris helps his bass notes along with a little body English.

LISA TANNER, 1980.

We're all kind of doing that, only we're joining the part of our minds that are devoted to music, which is something we don't fully understand—it's something that's intuitive and mysterious. (GS)

trevor rabin (1991): I don't know how this is going to work out. We're getting roadies, but we might need referees. (GS)

alan (1991): I thought it was going to be a lot more difficult than it has been. Bill and I are getting along extremely well, especially considering the different styles. Things will be worked out quite well for the stage. Certain numbers we've played already have really locked in so well—they are very powerful as a result of the dual drumming. It really has opened up opportunities—especially when you can give and take. You can really enhance the music. (WS)

bill (1994): The eight-man lineup wasn't much fun. I was there for decorative purposes only. One critic put it very well, I thought: He said that Alan White was the meat and potatoes and I was the hollandaise sauce.
   (1995): Steve also had some trouble fitting in with Trevor, because it was a nonstarter, really. The two of them couldn't really work together, there wasn't any space. It was as difficult as an idea as it was ludicrous. They couldn't find a common meeting ground in the guitar playing; they weren't being difficult—they tried. (TMI)

trevor rabin (1995): It was very much the two different camps. I got on very well with Bill and Rick and although Steve and I had differences of opinion of how things should be approached, we still got by okay. People think there was this animosity between us and there wasn't any, really. It was just difficult for the two of us. (TMI)

rick (1993): I can only speak for myself, but I thought it went really well. I went over with the sole intention of enjoying myself and having a good time. I felt from the word go that it would only happen once, so I wasn't interested in getting involved in any politics or arguments or opening any old wounds. I just had a really good time and I think that those who adopted the same attitude did the same. (TR)

eddie (1995): I didn't think the tour was that great. It just seemed that it was done for all the wrong reasons—for money, basically. (TMI)

WHY PETER BANKS DIDN'T PLAY WITH YES IN L.A. ON THE UNION TOUR

peter (1994): Tony asked me if I'd like to play a couple of tunes with them and I said I'd love to, providing we don't make a big deal out of it. That was promised and Tony talked to the other guys and they thought it was a great idea. I was just going to come out and play two encore pieces, "Roundabout" and something else ["Starship Trooper"]. It wasn't going to be rehearsed and I wasn't going to bring a guitar along. And there'd be a roadie to guide me to the stage and put a guitar in my hands and I'd be playing in the band. It would be as simple as that, no big deal. But it did get to be a bigger deal, everything with Yes ends up like that. It was announced on a couple of radio stations and people were calling me up asking for backstage passes. So on the day of the gig I'm in the backstage bar and I'm looking forward to it because I don't have to do anything. But about ten minutes before show time I was told I couldn't play, so I asked why and someone said, "Because Steve Howe doesn't want you to." I was very upset about the whole thing and just stayed in the bar and got very drunk. . . . It was very uncomfortable. When I saw Trevor Rabin in L.A. this year the first thing he did was to start apologizing for the Forum. I do think some of this might be political, because also at this time I was making overtures about suing [Atlantic for royalties]. And had I played with the band it would have established my position as a ex-member a lot stronger. (TMI)

steve (1994): I've never heard anything about that at all. I don't remember being asked if Peter could join us, I'm absolutely sure I wouldn't have minded. . . . There was an openness more from the European side [of Yes] about sharing this as a project, certainly making some special event [including Patrick Moraz, Geoff Downes, Trevor Horn] and I hope that would discount people from believing that I would elbow Peter from making an appearance, because I don't remember being questioned about it. (NFTE)

ON THEIR ROUTINES OR RITUALS BEFORE A SHOW

jon (1992): I started doing this about fifteen years ago where I would sleep before the show . . . well, not sleep, really, sort of hover, I'd just lie down and hover and start thinking about the goodness and the quality of life and how beautiful life really is. . . . During the show, you're in tune with the forces which surround, which is God. (COTM)

steve (1992): Now it's become important to me to get some sleep directly before a performance. I'll first work on my guitars for an hour or so, from five to six P.M. Then I'll check my equipment, and by seven I'll get very sleepy. From seven to seven forty-five, I'll close my eyes in the dressing room . . . it's more like a meditation than sleep because I don't actually drop off. When I wake up, all the anger that I might have had about the day is gone, and I feel confident and ready to go for the evening's performance. Basically, I use a method of relaxation through deep breathing, directing my breath to different parts of my body. (MT)

peter (1994): About half a bottle of brandy and that's about it! No, seriously, I never had any set routines, actually. The only thing I tried to do was get a little five or ten minutes' peace and quiet, which is almost impossible to do. (TMI)

trevor rabin (1995): I go to the toilet! That's about the only thing I do consistently every time. I don't play guitar before going on stage. I've never had that adrenaline or nervousness about going on stage. It's just never bothered me, I did piano competitions when I was six years old and even then it wasn't a problem. . . . I get on stage and I'm quite calm and if it's a good audience, by the third song I really play off the crowd. It spurs me on and I really get into it. I'm in another world on stage, it's like a religious experience to me. But it takes me time to warm up and there has been times where the audience has been kind of dead and it has affected my performance. (TMI)

alan (1994): I do a lot of stretching and warming up, because the last tour we did was a two-and-half-hour set and it was pretty much a go all the time. There was no solos or breaks for anybody, really, except very brief ones at the beginnings of numbers and things like that. It was a good workout, so I'd stretch a lot and I'd have a pair of sticks and do some rudiments on a counter, but nothing serious because we had a good warm-up on stage. We have a pretty long sound check. (TMI)

bill (1994): Now I warm up. I'm a drummer and drummers need blood in their fingers and wrists before they can start doing anything. So it's going to take you a half hour to practice and warm up. I have practice pads and I play with a metronome. I think of something fresh to do and I visualize myself playing and I try to think of different ways to play things. . . . It's pretty basic stuff, really. I try to remember not to rush, to breathe deep and be relaxed with the thing. Not so twenty-five years ago, I mean I didn't understand any of that. I just laid into the drums flat out. I didn't understand that you had to keep time and all that. It seemed really boring to me. (TMI)

chris (1991): When we're playing live, I'll usually be in the dressing room playing the first song we're about to do before we go on stage. However, there is one thing I like to warm up on sometimes, which is the track "Sound Chaser" from the *Relayer* album. (CSV)

geoff (1994): With Yes me and Alan used to do a couple of those really powerful ginsengs. So that used to make me feel a bit speedy. So we gave that up after a while. Alan got me into drinking the stuff and he said, "This will really set you down by the time you go on." But it actually made you feel a bit speedy. I stopped taking it, thinking, "It can't be a good thing for a drummer . . . if he starts speeding up I'll have to go with him!" I used to get pretty nervous, but I don't get nervous anymore. (TMI)

patrick (1995): I do some circular breathing exercises, some rhythmic exercising with my fingers before I go on stage. I do my best to be alone in my dressing room, as quiet as possible at least fifteen to twenty minutes before going on. And having done a very healthy sound check and playing for twenty minutes to a half an hour minimum at the sound check, which should take place no more than one hour to an hour and a half before I appear on stage. I don't eat anything and I don't drink any alcohol or take drugs. I go as straight as possible on stage and as relaxed as possible. (TMI)

PROBLEMS ON STAGE

steve (1991): I got into a mess at the Costa Mesa show because my line went down. I changed guitars and I just went into "The Ancient," thinking I hadn't played it in about three months! So I suddenly thought, "This is scaring the hell out of me, and I don't know what happens next." So I make my way and I get to "Leaves of Green" with a feeling of relief; I look around, anticipating that Jon would realize that I wanted him on stage to sing "Leaves of Green." I sort of held it here for a bit thinking, "Any second now" . . . well, Jon's dressing room may have been too far away! (YM)

peter (1994): Tony used to play a Vox Continental. The black keys were white and the white keys were black and that was the most distinctive thing about it. He tried to disguise it as a Hammond. But one night all of these pieces of cardboard just became unglued and collapsed and there was this Vox Continental on its spindly little legs.

When I was in Flash I had a roadie who always wanted to put strings on the guitar. And I said, "No, I'd rather put my own strings on." But for whatever reason on one gig he put the strings on and I didn't see the guitar because it was on stage. We used to have this opening music, Vaughn Williams which was about a minute and a half long and just when the music was ending we'd get on stage and pick up our instruments and start playing. So I pick up the guitar and there was this strange sensation like I thought that I'd forgotten how to play. Something was very wrong and I have a fear of not doing what you're supposed to do. It was like one of those nightmare things and I thought, "I've forgotten how to play. I don't know what to do!" I just sort of strummed the chords and this horrible sound came out. And what he had done was put the strings on the wrong way around, so the bottom E was where the top E should go. I yelled at him, "They're upside down, you bastard!" It was like a Spinal Tap thing. (TMI)

rick (1971): On one of my first gigs with Yes we were playing "Heart of the Sunrise." And there's one bit where there's a break and I have to come in [with the solo classical piano]. We finish the other bit and I'm meant to come straight in and there was dead silence. And I thought somebody's meant to play and they all know the piece very well . . . so it's got to be me. Think! And it suddenly occurred to me. The gap wasn't very long, it was only a few seconds, but it seemed like days. (SOY)

(1991): [On the Tormato tour] I remember the second night in Chicago when we went on stage . . . when you're moving you tend to look at the audience; you don't normally. There was a whole block in the front of about twenty seats that were empty and this was very strange because I knew the show was sold out. Now, with any show that is sold out with thousands of seats there are going to be twenty to thirty no-shows, it's a fact of life. But I thought this is really weird that there's twenty to thirty no-shows, but they're all in the front row—this is crazy! We came to the part of the show where Steve Howe played "Clap" and while he played we all used to disappear. I would jump off stage and go to where my road crew were. When I went under there . . . I'd never seen so many people in my life! And I said to my guy, "What on earth is going on?" He said, "The motor that turns the stage burned out. So we've taken twenty people from the front two rows." And *they* were underneath pushing the stage around! (UP)

alan (1994): There were some notes in like "And You and I" that were hard from Trevor Horn to hit. So we'd be playing a big gig and he'd start off at the front of the stage, but he knew the note was coming up so he'd end standing next to me at the back of the stage. He'd be standing on his tiptoes trying to make it and most nights he'd hit it, but he was scared of those notes. (TMI)

jon (1982): [In Pittsburgh on the Tormato tour someone ran up on stage and started choking Jon.] It was the funniest thing. Because when all the police came up on stage, they couldn't move. Because when that central point is a kind of focal point. On stage there are certain strong areas. It depends who is working there. If you've got Clapton on stage, the focal point is there. If a band is there, everybody's watching the band, but most eyes go to the singer. And being a central, circular stage, with another smaller stage in the middle—that point was like . . . burning. I've seen people come on stage, any kind of stage. And when you get to a certain point they start shaking. You've got a lot of people looking at you, for one thing. But the police got up on the center stage and they couldn't move. And there I was in the middle going, ''Now, look, guys, which way are we going?'' And the guy behind me [his attacker] was holding on, and I think he realized what he'd done. And he thought, ''Well, okay, I'm stoned, man. But what do I do now?'' So I said, ''Come on, everyone, get down,'' because they were all going to fall over at one point. They got to the edge of the stage and everybody calmed down. (R)

SOME OF THE WILD THINGS THAT CAN HAPPEN ON THE ROAD

ed sciaky, Philly DJ and close friend of the band (1982): In Jackson, Mississippi, some guys from a high school paper wanted to interview them and they were giving them a hard time, so I said, ''Look, let them come up! Meet people! Talk to people!'' So these real naive guys came up—Rick was hiding behind the curtains and was . . . relieving himself . . . it was really stupid and obnoxious, but it was also pretty funny.

I remember one tour when Brian [Lane] and I don't know who instigated the ''knights of the royal'' something-or-other, and everyone put their napkins on their heads, pouring half-and-half over their heads. Then people started throwing grapes and things; it was a really silly tour.

In 1977 we had the ''Yes Tour Awards'' where Rick came out dressed in his underwear and a banner on. It was a spaced-out night! (R)

alan (1994): Rick never liked *Topographic Oceans*. On the tour we'd be playing away and he'd have a twelve-pack of beer and he was eating an Indian curry on stage while he was playing! But we all kept smelling this curry and we looked over and saw Rick eating while he was playing some intricate part from *Topographic Oceans*. It was pretty ridiculous.

There's this promoter in England called Harvey Goldsmith. And we were playing in Glasgow and Rick would do things like tell Harvey to come into the dressing room and he'd balance the salad dish on the door. When Harvey came through the door he got drenched with the whole thing! Rick was the prankster. (TMI)

trevor rabin (1995): When we started the Union tour Rick began doing his solo spot from ''Catherine Parr.'' He was playing it and the next day I thought, ''I'm going to play that with him.'' So I got up on stage and started playing it to him and he stopped and said, "What is that?" And someone replied, "Trevor is playing it on guitar," and Rick said, "He can't do that . . . you bastard! Now you have to play it with me in the show." The only thing was every couple of shows, he'd do it as fast as he possibly could, but it is a really difficult guitar riff and I'd be really challenged to keep up. (TMI)

steve (1993): We came off stage in Quebec [on the Union tour] and everyone was ecstatic. We were really hot that night . . . in a massive stadium in Quebec. When we came off stage, we had done only one encore. I said, "We're not going to leave these people with one encore." The show for other reasons was a little bit intense, but it was marvelous. So I went to the corridor and got in my car. Then I got out of my car and went back down the corridor and I said, "Look, guys, I can hear them in my car and I'm not leaving." They said, "No way, we are not doing another encore." The seven of them. So I got back in my car and I drove off. And they went on and did an encore without me! I was so mad! (MNN)

trevor rabin (1995): Chris gets a terrible cringe on his face whenever he hears about anything to do with cuts on a hand—he goes nuts! So what we did on the last show of the Union tour was Alan got one of those trick blades that you put on your finger and it looks like it's almost cut off. We got some tomato sauce for it and it looked really authentic. I went up to Chris and said, "Where's Benny?"—who was our tour manager. And he asked why and I just acted really anxious, saying, "We need Benny, RIGHT NOW!" And he said, "But what's wrong?" I told him, "I'm not going to tell you, because you'll freak out. I've got to get back to the dressing room." So he followed me curiously and walked in and then saw Alan with his finger cut up. Chris didn't even make a sound, he just left the room white in the face. I ran out to him and said, "Hey, we're only joking," and he shouted, "You bastard!" He got me back later by injecting water into the seat I used when I played my guitar solo. So when I sat down my butt was completely wet! I had to keep playing, but it did kind of screw up the performance. It was difficult to focus when suddenly your pants are wet. (TMI)

steve (1994): On the Topographic tour we had all that scenery on stage. We had a road crew that was quite used to equipment, but scenery to them was rubbish! This wasn't gear, you couldn't plug it in. There was all of this fiberglass and things lying around and we had this tunnel that brought us on to the stage. My roadie Claude at the time was a bit wild and they hated it so much that they smashed it up one day! They just got so cross with it, it got in everybody's way. But there again Claude would get very protective of my guitars, if anyone would get near them he'd start to bark. The crew is the part of the show that doesn't really get mentioned. In a way they were a part of the source of humor for a lot of things. They would invade us at hotel food rooms. They were generally rowdies; we weren't really like that so much. We sort of laughed and looked on.

When we finished tours there was an unpredictability about what would happen the last night. Last nights were intrepid, they were hazardous. One night I had my amazing moccasins on and they were covered in beads and

I got hit with cream pies! The shoes went into a plastic bag for a while hoping that I could find something to do with them—to get rid of this cream. (TMI)

geoff (1994): It was, I suppose, my first entry into the rock 'n' roll scene. So I did things that were fairly rock 'n' roll. I remember charging down Sunset Strip in an open-topped Cadillac, standing on the seat—which probably wasn't a good idea. I was shouting something about Rommel at the time. It was in a limo and I had my head out the top, climbing out, and I was on the roof. . . . That was pretty wild. (TMI)

eddie (1995): The band were pretty much married and faithful and it was really just Alan and me that used to have a wild time. He and I were the bachelors. I remember one time when we had played a huge arena that I invited the whole audience back to the hotel for a party! Oh, my God, it was a madhouse! You couldn't even get to your room, the place was packed.

As far as rock bands go we were pretty mild in some ways. I do remember setting up Chris's room in an empty swimming pool. I threw it in and then perfectly set it up in the pool. He was pretty pissed! (TMI)

THE BAND:

"OUR REASON

TO BE HERE"

Yes has been a special entity since its inception. All of its members will attest to the profound experience of being in the band. Of course they also have strong opinions about the music they created, their band mates, and themselves.

ON BEING IN YES

bill (1995): The band Yes encompasses every conceivable extreme known to mankind. It's crazy, isn't it?

You could say the band was a success, because it was the sum of its faults as these things often are. And if you corrected all the faults in Yes, you would have had a really horrible group. (TMI)

steve (1994): I saw a picture the other day that almost made me cry. It was a photo of Jon, Chris, and I singing on stage around 1971–72 and you could see that we were tight, harmonizing and creating together. We were the artistic nucleus of Yes, no matter whether we had Bill and Tony, or Rick and Alan, or Patrick. But I was upset because it reminded me of a time when we were all leaders in Yes. Then, when you get people saying "I'm Yes" or "My song has got to be on the album," it all goes wrong. This pushing to be out in front and on top has nothing [to do] with what Yes was once about. Yes was all about that photo, with the three of us working together. And on top of that, we had the best keyboard player and the best drummer in the world. (GTRSP)

(1972): I don't think at first America was quite ready for this, a group that came on and didn't wiggle our bottoms too much and didn't grin very much. This has put some people off, but by the end of the set, I think most are convinced of our convictions: that we are dedicated and that we would still be playing even if we were stuck living in broken-down surroundings, which we've all been through, where you didn't have anything to hang on to except your music. Still, we feel we want to get the standard even higher for our music. Jon Anderson once said, "Instead of people clapping at the end, we don't want them to be able to clap, like we really did it to them." In England, somebody said, "Yes play music, and the things they play together are things people don't normally play together." Like we play two things together at once which are harmonically right. We've got a bass player who often plays a kind of top line lead, and a drummer who is very rarely content to just play a straight beat. He usually figures in with the whole rhythm of the song and the bass player a lot and Rick and I have a fairly easy job of just using our imaginations and overlaying the right kind of expression on top of it all. (G)

rick (1974): I think one of the things we are aiming for is when somebody says to you, "Yes, you think of the music, not the five individuals in the band." If you think back to the old days to the great writers like Mozart and Beethoven, and you say Beethoven, you don't think of a deaf gray-haired man sitting down and writing a piece of music, you think of his music. I believe that's what you've got to aim for. (DB)

(1989): We all feel that you should be able to listen to a piece of music and enjoy it. If you just want to listen once when it's on the radio, that's great. If, however, the mood takes you to get a bit more out of it, then there's no reason why you shouldn't be able to put headphones on and go deeper into the music. And if that depth hasn't been planted there by the musicians, you can't go looking for it. It's like trying to scuba dive in three feet of water. (K)

patrick (1994): As a rock 'n' roll band, Yes could be considered the Stravinsky of rock 'n' roll. (YV)

[They were] sometimes impenetrable. Not Alan, but Jon, Steve, and Chris were sometimes the prima donnas of impenetration. You could not decipher or comprehend them. . . . But they had a solid knowledge of their instruments and an extreme bravery to play what they wanted. (TMI)

bill (1994): I think we were five lost little troopers, really. We were all beginners at music and we all grew up in Yes. Yes was our first love affair and it was our first girlfriend. And we learned about music in Yes and we learned about ourselves and you can't really ask for more. There are those among us who would like to make changes to themselves as a result of having been in Yes, me included. There are lots of things in Yes when I listen to it that I hate about myself that I've tried to iron out in my playing, and that's often what musicians do. They use music as a mirror, you hold it up and you see yourself laughingly clearly, and you then may wish to make changes as you see fit. Or you can keep making the same mistakes endlessly if you want. And I think some people have come further than others. (TMI)

peter (1994): It was a long time ago when I was in the band. It's like looking through an old scrapbook of photos or going to a high school reunion. It's something I did a long time ago and I have good memories about it and bad memories about it, but I don't miss it. (YV)

rick (1993): It's like a nice kind of cancer. You've got it and it never goes away. It lies dormant, then every now and then it comes back to life. (TR)

geoff (1994): For me being a sort of novice and being brought in at that level, I found the experience as being completely bizarre. I would imagine bands as revered as Pink Floyd and Yes were really together and really straight and organized. But it amazed me how unorganized everything was and yet when it came to the actual gig and the records and stuff, everything just fell into place. It was very strange. The gigs were great, but the whole infrastructure was very fragile . . . to use a term from the past. (TMI)

alan (1991): I've always considered myself part of what might be called the "egg," or the nucleus of Yes. Yes is a fulcrum. People have joined and departed since I've been with the band. It's an ongoing situation. Now, you might say that people have come back to the nest, as it were. (YY)

rick (1977): Yes was much more into the music than the Strawbs, but their social life was virtually nonexistent. Also the food thing: The Strawbs all ate together and we'd go out and have a drink together. But with Yes, at the time [1972–74], well, no one ever sort of had a drink. They were all on health food—not completely, but most of the time. (RS)

trevor rabin (1992): Chris and Jon, they are so totally different. You would never think they would be in a band together, because they are so different. Chris goes to bed at seven in the morning and Jon gets up at nine, so their clocks are totally different. And Jon's cosmic, if you like, for want of a better expression, and Chris likes to party. In a lot of bands they are a tight unit and everyone does the same things, they go to the same parties. That's really NOT how this band is . . . everyone has a very different lifestyle and enjoys different things. But we're just as close as the bands that do have those things in common. (ITS)

eddie (1973): I never thought they would make it, though, that's for sure. I thought they were just too far out of line of music that was being bought. It was a great shock to me when their albums got in the charts. (RS)
   (1992): There were a lot of different factions in Yes, and they had contrary tastes and feelings about the music. I would try to channel all this high energy

of wanting to do everything and act as a mediator, a referee, trying to figure out what ideas were good and which were bad. (M)

trevor horn (1980): Doing things that no one else does is really what Yes is all about. The exceptional thing about Yes was that they could always make those incredibly complex records and reproduce them on stage. They really cared about what they did. I know that in the early days Yes practically bankrupted themselves, so they could get ahold of a decent PA system. They were the first band ever in England to be miked up through a sound system as opposed to the sound of the band coming off stage and the singer coming through the speakers. Yes was the first band in England to have everything coming through a huge PA system. They cared about putting the music across so it sounded good live. There were no passengers in Yes, people could always play really well and in a very unique way. (R)

bill (1991): With this band, all we have to do is turn up on stage—and not fight—and the people are thrilled. We don't even have to play a single note and they go absolutely wild. I'd say that's a way to make a living, eh? (K)

chris (1976): We've had, enjoyed, and probably will do a longer life, because we're not limited to the syndrome of we're only as good or as popular as our next record. (I)

alan (1995): People in bands are all the same kind of characters. Bass players are always slow and late for anything. They always stop things midstream and want to pontificate on something. Guitarists are very temperamental. If something doesn't satisfy them, they fly off the handle. It's because of all the notes that they play. Lead singers are complete extroverts. They want to change everything all the time, "I need to change the lyrics here . . ." Keyboard players are kind of mediators to an extent. That's the role they play. If you're really pissed off at someone, tell the keyboard player and the other guy is bound to find out about it. But drummers are the real crazies. They are total eccentrics.

(1994): In the never-ending search for new things and new developments you can't be in a better band than Yes. Yes is the kind of band that doesn't look at the horizon, it looks over it. Yes music is a timeless thing. (TMI)

ON COMPOSING YES MUSIC

jon (1991): I think we are all into uplifting music. Personally I didn't follow the Rolling Stones into the satanic realm, I followed the Beatles into "All You Need Is Love." That was my dream and I loved it and I tended to follow that train of thought. We're sort of driven to write this kind of music, it's not even soul searching. It's very spirited music in many ways. (UP)

chris (1991): I think the Yes theme has always been a hopeful one. I think we've used dark expressionism in order to show the difference between light and dark. But usually if the song refers to darkness, there's a positive attitude at the end of it. (UP)

rick (1989): We'll play around with a piece of music and Jon will come up with a rough line or a simple sequence on guitar. I'll change the chord sequences around in different inversions, and then Jon will start singing. It might be the nature of the way I play that encourages Jon to come in at one or another point. That tends to dictate the meter of the piece, because I'll have to change something to adapt to where Jon comes in. When you look at it, it means I'm playing ⁴/₄, ⁵/₄, ⁷/₈, ⁵/₄—something like that. Phrasing is very important. Sometimes, at the end of a phrase, you'll want to go very quickly to the next phrase, and that might chop a ⁴/₄ bar to ⁷/₈ or ³/₄. But it's never deliberate. we've never said, "Let's be real clever." It always stems from how it feels. Oftener than not, we'll record it down, and then somebody will go, "What bloody time signature is that?" (K)

jon (1994): The idea of strong melody came from one classical composer called Stravinsky. Stravinsky made music, which was being made by lots of people. Very similar, very avant-garde, but he retained something that they didn't, and that was the melodies. And if you listen to any Stravinsky he holds it all together with melody and I never wanted to lose that. I was more of the melodious type, where the guys in the band would be off and running with all these ideas, figurative licks, out of that I realized if it all went that way we'd have a Mahavishnu of sorts. (ITS)

(1971): After we've put the song together and recorded it, I start to look at the thing as a whole and decide there is a meaning to it—if I can find a meaning. And possibly the people who listen to it will find different meanings. (SOY)

steve (1981): All of a sudden I suppose we had this cause. We were trying to be very progressive; no twelve bars, no "this" sort of guitar, not "that" sort of drumming. (R)

bill (1994): There was very much a feeling in the band that real musicians composed music. That it wasn't enough to be a drummer and it wasn't enough to be a guitar player or a bass player, but it certainly wasn't enough to be a drummer. And that real people composed music, wrote music. This was the big thing, you know, Lennon-McCartney. If you were a band in London instead of Lennon-McCartney, you had your Anderson-Squire or whatever it was. And Jon was always on me, quite aggressively to write music. I was glad that he did, but not everybody is a natural composer. So I noodled around at the piano and started my career as a composer, which is very negligible, really. Just as someone would produce the odd line or riff or idea for a harmony or something. I've become much better at it since. I would occasionally come with a line that would earn me a small credit. (TMI)

ON JON ANDERSON

Jon Anderson is known all over the world for his spiritual, mystical music and his distinctive voice. His songs are filled with positive energy and spiritual love and have reached millions of devoted fans. Jon is constantly working on several projects simultaneously: solo albums, collaborations (such as with

Vangelis, Kitaro, and Mike Oldfield), movie soundtracks, ballets, and symphonic works. His remarkable creative drive touches the hearts and souls of fans all around the world with his beloved music.

jon (1989): I'm a musician. I'm an artiste. I'm forty-four, I'm halfway through my career, and I'm still trying to discover the art of making good music that will last at least, well . . . longer than two months anyway. So much music these days is computerized, commuterized, saturized, businesswised. (Q)

ON JON'S DAILY SCHEDULE

jon (1994): I wake up. I meditate. I'm very in tune with keeping fit. I like to go for a walk. And I write some music on a piano. Review the work I'm going to do that day. Have a light breakfast. Then go back to bed for an hour, maybe. Just rest. Get ready for the day. The day can consist of a zillion things at once. It's a question of balancing everything out. I tend to want to do two or three things a day. When I'm not working, I'm traveling. And when I'm traveling I tend to read. I enjoy reading books and I love listening to Sibelius. I listen to Sibelius whenever I can. I love Frederick Delius. I love to read Henry Miller and Carlos Castaneda. . . . Dreaming is really where I get into the mysteries of life. I love my dreams very much. I've been practicing dreaming now for about ten years. There's an art to dreaming. You can find books about it. You can wake up in your dreams. You can have focused discussions with people in your dreams. Life is a dream, really. But it's a physical one. But when you are in your sleeping dream, it is a highly spiritual one. (YM)

ON JON'S SINGING

jon (1978): I don't actually like my voice too well. I felt that way until a couple of years ago, when I realized I was being able to make better statements with the voice, whereas on the earliest two or three albums, I was so unsure of my voice. I really used to shake in the studio. The lyrical side is very important for the sort of notes that you hit, sometimes. It's very hard to hit a top D with "w" sound, like "what" or "were." But with a "d" and "a," like "danced," you can hit top D with it, because there is a strong first sound, but with "w" you have to spread your mouth 'round it more, so you tend to hit high notes on certain lyrics. But I would never sit down and assess that when I'm writing. (MM)

trevor rabin (1987): The thing that makes Yes sound like Yes more than anything is Jon's voice. You could put any band there, to a degree, and it would sound like Yes. (GW)

rick (1989): Jon's voice is so bizarre that you can put down the kitchen sink on tape. You could put down the musical spectrum so that there isn't a gap in sight, and still his voice will cut through it all. You can also put down something extraordinarily delicate like a piano or a solo acoustic guitar: He'll sing in the same mode and somehow it'll match perfectly. (K)

Jon takes a break from touring for a game of "football"—English style—in Philadelphia.

peter (1994): He's a strange singer, because his voice is very frail. He doesn't have a loud voice, it is a very fragile voice. One thing I remember is if we were working a lot, doing five or six dates in a row, his voice would get stronger. The more tired he would get the stronger his voice would get, which is very unusual for singers. And it was the same recording as well. Usually when you record a singer they're good for about an hour and after an hour forget it. Every singer I've worked with is like that. With Jon it was different, we'd start recording and there was this little squeak. After he got tired and had sang this thing again and again his voice would all of a sudden get better.

jonathan elias (1991): All you have to do is have his drink of lemon, hot water, and some honey ready for him; turn the mike on and he sings away. Jon gets a little specific about some of the echoes and some of the delays that are on his voice while he's singing. He likes to have a very crystalline . . . chamber happening and get into his vibe. His vibe consists of candles and things like that and Jon really needs it in order to get into his space. Then it's a matter of letting him do a few takes. (MN)

ON JON'S LYRIC WRITING

jon (1992): I don't think about it. I have a general need for clarity in my life and to express my opinions about what my life is aspiring to. And I hope that somebody else feels the same way. More than ever, I just let the spirit flow and write down what comes. I never felt so much that I was a poet but just a writer of ideas. Then sometimes I look at it and realize that it is poetry. It does have a balance and a literary point of view. It had substance. I never tried to create that, it just happened. So I realized I was being well used and I was a good vehicle for words and expression. It just seemed to happen naturally. (COTM)

eddie (1995): I always loved the way Jon wrote his lyrics. The rest of the band gave him such a hard time about his lyrics. They'd all say to him, "Jon, your fucking lyrics don't make any sense at all! What is this river, mountain stuff—it's absolutely meaningless drivel!" And he'd say, "Look, when I'm writing lyrics I use the words like colors. I use words for the sounding of the words, not the actual meaning." Chris especially used to tease him like hell. (TMI)

ON THE WAY JON PRESENTED HIS IDEAS TO THE BAND

bill (1992): Usually he presented them with a great deal of vigor, a great deal of muscle and a great deal of "If you don't like it, think of something better." That was usually Jon's approach. So he would play something really, horrendously terrible and most people would say, "Ohhh . . . groan. Do we have to play this? Oh, no! Well, all right, if we've got to . . . why don't you put the sixth there in the chord and play it like that?" And then someone else would say, "Yeah, if you put an F in the bass instead of the G root, then it will sound better . . ." and you see what happens, the original idea would be turned into music by the four competent musicians around him. So he would bang out some horrendous, god-awful noise over one chord, getting his fingers caught in the strings, with a look in his eyes that said, "Quit or make it better." Which is a technique that Hitler would use. Somewhere slightly to the right of Hitler. (ITS)

trevor rabin (1995): I didn't really get to know Jon until the end of the first tour. We went out for pizza one night and had a couple of drinks and loosened up together after the show and got to know each other a little bit. I realized, "He's all right." Before that night I'd heard what everyone has heard about Jon being Napoleon and a megalomaniac. Obviously that's there! But I get on fine with him. . . . There is friction at times, but there should be friction. We've never had major problems. . . . And I saw how musical he was, forgetting about his vision, lyrics, personality, and what he stands for—just purely from a musical standpoint I got to see that he is VERY musical. He's obviously not a schooled musician, but I think Jon's ear is amazing. (TMI)

peter (1994): He always had a great sense of melody. I remember he wanted to be Joe Cocker at one time. He went through a phase of not only wanting to sing like Joe Cocker, which was obviously impossible for him to do, but he went through the Joe Cocker sort of motions, which I found hilarious. . . . We were a very loud band, but that quiet voice always seemed to cut through. (TMI)

patrick (1995): Everyone thinks Jon Anderson is God and so on and he's not. He's just like a struggling musician, like we all are. He's got great talent, he's got some inventive sequences . . . he was always very vague, nothing defined because it has to be defined. He's got a very strong willpower like Napoleon. He does have an interesting voice, the voice of Yes. But God he is not!(TMI)

bill (1994): I think he's a man of terrific strength and phenomenal stamina. There is an unattractive side and an extremely attractive side to it. Somehow he's managed to keep himself on top, even when he wasn't in it, I think. Somehow you had the feeling that he was central to everything.

(1995): I can feel more affinity with a Frenchman than with someone from Accrington [Jon's hometown in the north of England], which is some god-forsaken part of the country that I've never penetrated and have no intention of ever penetrating.

Jon always seemed so frustrated as a musician, because he couldn't explain himself. It would have been great if he'd had a little technical understanding. If he had some idea of why the keyboard player chose that inversion or why anything worked or why the rhythm could go this way, but it could also go that way. Any of those things . . . I always sensed he would have been a happier guy. But had he been a happier guy it probably would have been a horrible band, you know? He had no technical understanding at all of how music works. He thought if you bang at it, if you shout loud enough it will work. Music doesn't work that way, you have to let music occur. You have to get out of the way of it occurring. Forget that you know how to do a paradiddle, forget that you know all those scales that Rick Wakeman knows. Then the music has some chance of coming alive. I always felt sorry for Jon, because I wished that he could express himself more. I always wanted him to be a happier guy and to shout a little less. He would just bang the table really hard and bang the rehearsal room a lot to get this stuff out. And it came, because people got pissed off with it. He'd drive people crazy and shout so much that people would say, "Okay Jon, we'll do it your way."

He'd always make these diatonic movements on the piano—the white notes only. I remember one day taking two or three of his fingers and putting them on the black notes. And I said, "Look, press them down with some white notes! They'll sound great." It was a charming moment, actually. He put his fingers on the black notes and pressed them down with some white notes and he didn't like them. They were new chords to his ears and he didn't really like them. He did like all black notes, but a mix of the two . . . he couldn't trust himself there. His world got too complex if you were going to mix the blacks and the whites. And I thought, "What a shame, because in his ears he's only hearing diatonic white notes. Not any accidentals or mistakes." To me the accidentals is where it begins. The sharps and the flats. Most of his melodies were based on this common scale and once in a while a passing chord would appear from Steve Howe or Rick Wakeman, which was great! And sometimes within these limitations nice things would happen, but for me I need more black notes in there.

(1994):It was him that got the band off the ground in terms of getting in a van, getting petrol in the van, getting concerts, getting one place or the other. He was the guy who hassled on the phone in the first instance. He was a driven man. He knew what he wanted. He didn't know how to get to Manchester, but he knew he needed a concert in Manchester. He was the organizational thing just by sheer force of willpower and the music was the way. He'd do the music the same way. (TMI)

eddie (1995): Everyone always criticizes Jon for his lack of musical training, but in fact I think that's one of his beauties. That he didn't follow set structures when he was writing, he was like, "Oh, I'll just throw that there," for no apparent reason, and it turned out to be good. (TMI)

jon (1989): Napoleon. The hippie with the iron hand. That's what they used to call me, though I think I'm more of a sergeant-major now, I like having Lead Singer's Disease. I have to let the others know I'm listening. (Q)

rick (1994): Jon gave the best description of himself to me, better than anyone else could do. He said, "I am the only man who is fighting to save this planet while living on another!" (YIS)

ON CHRIS SQUIRE

Chris Squire is called the "Keeper of the Flame" by Yes fans for his role in keeping the band going for over twenty-six years (and appearing on every Yes album—a feat that no one else has accomplished). He is the calm center of Yes. Nothing much seems to faze him and that is probably how he has managed to keep the group around for so long. Chris is known for having a very high standard of excellence that he expects his work to live up to. His bass playing is a fine example of the Squire excellence; he is considered by many to be one of the most outstanding and influential bassists in rock music.

chris (1976): A lot of my music and my playing has developed on a grand scale with a very monumental feeling. I don't think that's all I'm capable of, of course, because I can do much subtler things as well. But at this period in my life, I'm very into powerful music—not power in the sense of sheer volume, but in respect to dynamic power. Much of it comes from the things I used to enjoy when I was younger—with the choir, the huge pipe organ, and the guys with the straight trumpets. You can't help but be moved by that type of music, just because of the massive power behind it. I'm not really talking about the ''Hallelujah Chorus'' type of thing, because I have a taste for a slightly more medieval form of music. You might call it epic music, but I don't have a one-track mind about it. (BRG)

(1991): I like changing things from the ordinary and then coming up with a strange tuning or a different way of doing things. [Making] a song that will make people go, ''That's different. How did they do that?'' (CSV)

(1976): I follow the vocal a lot in what I play. Not directly, of course, but I like to use it as a center, playing in, out, and around it. I find that I usually relate more to the basic melody line of the song than to what's going on in the middle—the chords and all. (BRG)

(1994): During the seventies and early eighties, I was known as a person who played a lot of notes; after Trevor joined on *90125*, we were doing slightly more rock 'n' roll–oriented material, so I happily changed my style

Chris Squires away some reading material in a Japan Airport.

to fit that. Now I'm kind of combining both styles again. Overall, I feel, as I always have, that the bass should be an equal voice in the band—not lead or background, per se, just an integral part of the music. (BP)

(1973): One could basically say that Jon and I tend to run the group because we were both behind it in the beginning. We conceived it in the beginning. The decisions have fallen on us more than anyone. (RS)

(1992): I used to read a lot. I go in and out of watching TV. Sometimes I go through periods of watching different kinds of TV and becoming very media aware. And then usually when I'm going into a project or something like that I cannot watch TV at all. I listen to the radio a lot too. I seem to just be kind of a social person, I like people and most of the time I do think about music.(WS)

geoff (1994): My own perception of being in Yes was that Chris was actually the quiet controlling influence of the band. There hasn't been a version of Yes that hasn't included Chris Squire. I think the selection of people has often been down to him. That he is the quiet motivator and he's the one who has kept the group going through thick and thin, so I admire him for that. Particularly with the kind of egos that are in a band of Yes's caliber, where the instrumentalists are very high profile.

Chris I have a lot of respect for. He was a very capable person to imagine how Yes should be. He was probably best qualified to dictate what Yes should be. And he was also very encouraging to me, who had really come into the situation pretty green. The first gig that I did with Yes was in front of eighteen thousand people in Toronto. He was very understanding and gave me a lot of encouragement, "You can do it!" And Alan was the same. I think it stems from being a nonstandard sort of rhythm section. They had a kind of sixth sense between them for where to put the beat, it was almost an involuntary reflex the way they played together. That was encouraging, to have such a solid rhythm section playing under you . . . it gave me quite a lot of freedom to stretch out. (TMI)

steve (1982): Chris was stronger and more forthcoming than any bass player I'd ever worked with. He had ideas. Here was just a multitude of ideas—that's what was so good. (R)

bill (1995): It always took him a long time, but he always thought out a nice bass movement. This wasn't rock 'n' roll bass playing, he thought up nice, genuinely good movements. A little like church music, the bass in some of those parts, I think. I thought they were really good. He took his time, Jesus, he took his time! But he would eventually get there. Just when the rehearsal was finishing, it ended at five o' clock and the hands were nearly on five to five and you thought this hell would eventually end in five minutes . . . you'd got a decent part and you could record the tune tomorrow, Chris would say, "I'm not happy with this. Why don't we . . ." and we'd sit there another two hours! But it would get better and we'd all have to grudgingly admit that after several hours with Squire it had got better. (TMI)

eddie (1995): Chris actually was the most perfectionist in the band, musically. And I think to be honest with you that's one reason why Bill left, because Chris wanted everything to be charted out—especially the kick drum and bass. And Bill wanted a bit more freedom. If anyone did take time in the studio it was Chris and sometimes it did drive me crazy a bit, but it all came out right in the end. Chris is a great guy and I love him to death. He's very cool. (TMI)

trevor rabin (1995): In the studio Trevor Horn used to say, "Get the slippers out, we're doing bass tonight!" Chris would listen to an overdub and say, "On the third note there seems to be a funny noise." And we'd listen back and tell him, "No, there's not! No one's going to hear that." He picks up on everything and it takes ages. But I've played with many great bass players and I can tell you there's nothing like playing live with Chris. It's like having this maniac elephant next to you with a turbo charge. He's quite amazing. He's never been one who cares if he has the Jaco Pastorius technique or not, he says, "I do what I do." He has his own style and it's amazing to play with it. The power is incredible. I call his playing "quite confident." When he's hit a note, you know he's hit it! (TMI)

trevor horn (1980): Chris is very clever. He's never a guy to be taken lightly. He's a great visionary. (R)

trevor rabin (1995): He is like a brother [to me] and I mean that almost in a literal sense. . . . If anyone says anything bad about Chris I go nuts. I love the guy dearly. (TMI)

patrick (1995): He is a true artist. Chris is a true rock 'n' roll star. (TMI)

peter (1994): He is a good bass player. He's a very unusual bass player, he wouldn't often go for the root chord. If you were playing an A major he might go for a D or G note or something like that. He would not go for the obvious, which was very good. His timing was always good, but he would tend to slow things down, as he does with everything! (TMI)

bill (1994): Chris Squire was generally the conductor of Yes and he still is. He on a whole prefers playing with Alan to me because Alan will do whatever he wants with the tempo. It's interesting, but it makes for an uncomfortable kind of rhythm. If you ever try to play percussion with those two—which I have—it's a nightmare, because you don't know what the tempo's going to do. It never settles. If Squire decides that he wants it to sound a little more pompous and a bit more dragged out, then he will, he'll drag it out till death do us part. (TMI)

jon (1994): A lot of the musical things over the years would have gone too light but for Chris. Chris sort of brings it back down to earth, because he's a Pisces and has that sort of earth/water energy. It does take a long time to get things coordinated in his mind, but I think that's a very good situation, because I just tend to just fly away. I come up with ideas very fast. But it's always been a little battle as to how it finishes up, how it all turns out. Me with a zillion ideas and him with a more decisive point of view. (ITS)

(1989): I love Chris and I will work with him again, but for years he's been late for everything. Rehearsals starting at two and he'd never be there till five. (Q)

SOME OF THE MANY "CHRIS SQUIRE LATE STORIES"

peter (1994): In the Syn we went to pick Chris up. We were going to a gig in Stoke-on-Trent which was about one hundred miles away. He was always traditionally late and he had this girlfriend whose name was Sheila who would make excuses for him. And we'd wait for about a half an hour while he got out of the bath or finished his breakfast or whatever. This could be happening midday, one o'clock in the afternoon, or something like that. But this one time, we had been waiting outside because we weren't invited in, something snapped and someone just said, "Let's go without him." And we did. We went to this place in the Midlands and we did the gig without a bass player to teach him a lesson. It didn't work, it didn't make any difference whatsoever. I think he was a little hurt about it. He said, "Why did you go without me?" He wasn't angry, but he said, "I was nearly ready." That was always his line. (TMI)

alan (1994): We've left Chris a couple of times because he's so late. We were on a private plane in Vienna or somewhere like that. We got up and were all waiting for Chris at the hotel and we were waiting in the limos and heard that Chris was still in the bathtub. So we left and waited on the plane for another half hour again. We sat there and finally made the decision to just leave him. So we flew to Rotterdam and got there, but apparently Chris was only ten minutes behind us when we took off. He then had to take a flight with some of the higher-up roadies—lighting guys and stuff like that. They had to make the same journey and they were on a small Cessna plane and it was the worst flight of the whole tour. Chris had to spend an hour and a half to two hours with all of these roadies bouncing up and down all over the sky. He got to the other end and he was just furious. But he was never late on the tour ever again. He was there before anyone else. (TMI)

geoff (1994): I remember Chris coming to play once in just his underpants, because one of the roadies had packed his clothes and had put his trousers in as well. So Chris turned up at the sound check with this big long jacket on, with his spindly hairy legs sticking out of the bottom.

We were an hour late going on stage, because Chris was asleep in his hotel room and he'd locked the door and left the phone off the hook. So they had to get the fire department to go in and break the door down with one of the hotel managers. They got him out and on stage about an hour late. And then he just started playing, you know? (TMI)

trevor rabin (1995): We were at a gig and Chris wasn't there and we were supposed to go on in twenty minutes. No one knew where he was. Finally our tour manager called over to the hotel and he was in his room. We were playing at the Madison Square Garden and the hotel is a considerable distance away from it. Our tour manager told him, "Chris, you're going on in a few minutes! Get down here!" And Chris's response was, "Well, I've just ordered dinner." (TMI)

chris (1993): In reality I may get somewhere at the last minute, but I'm actually not late. Although I have been a couple of times. It's a joke that I've always had with them. One of the many reasons I tend to be late is that I hate waiting for people. It's kind of selfish of me, really, but I don't do it to be difficult. Of course, a lot of people react to that and tell me to be there half an hour before the time they mean. Then when I get there and wait for half an hour, I'm thinking, "Where is everybody?" (WS)

ON PETER BANKS

After Peter Banks left Yes he went on to a variety of different projects. He formed Flash and they recorded three albums together before management and personnel problems broke the group up. He then did a lot of session work and producing through the seventies and eighties before embarking on a solo career.

Peter has since released two fine albums. *Instinct* and *Self-Contained*, which feature his unique blending of musical styles and his wonderfully fluid guitar playing.

peter (1994): [on becoming a solo artist] I had no idea of doing a solo album at all. I'd done one in 1973 [*The Two Sides Of Peter Banks*] and was only fifty percent happy with the way it came out. Capitol Records wanted to release both my solo album and the third Flash album at the same time; which was ridiculous really, because what happened was that both records suffered from the decision. I'd always had bits and pieces of music, which I've recorded for my own amusement, really. I never thought about doing a solo record, mainly because rock instrumental albums are notoriously difficult to market. At the time I was living in L.A. and it seemed like every guitar player was bringing out instrumental albums—it was flourishing. A lot of these were sent to me and most of them didn't impress me. And I started thinking, "Well, I could do better than that!" And *Instinct* evolved out of that.

I'm a bit of a music junkie. When I go into a record store it's bad news. I've got so many things in my collection—there's things that I haven't even listened to! (TMI)

tony (1985): Peter Banks was definitely an emotional player; not that he was a blues player, but he was very experimental, and not automatic at all. (K)

jon (1994): Peter Banks, [was] a very good guitar player, but his scope was sort of limited at times. (ITS)

alan (1994): I never worked with Peter Banks, but I have got to know him over the years. In fact I just saw him recently at the Yes Fest. He's a pretty nice guy, but again I've never actually played with him. He seems competent on the early records. (TMI)

bill (1995): He had a bit of jazz in him, a bit of Wes Montgomery and a lot of Pete Townshend. (TMI)

ON BILL BRUFORD

Bill Bruford has achieved near-legendary status in progressive rock for being the only musician to have been a member of the three seminal bands of the seventies: Yes, King Crimson, and Genesis. He went on to help form the widely respected group UK and to put out his own jazz fusion records (with his bands Bruford and Earthworks). Bill is known not only as a world-class percussionist, but for his artistic integrity which has remained intact all of these years.

bill (1994): I love seeing the whites of an audience's eyes instead of being stuck in the back and seeing John Wetton's ass. Life for me is a series of asses that I played behind. Adrian Belew has got a very nice ass, slim. John Wetton's is a little bigger. Jon Anderson's is very small. Nice legs, lousy ass. It's a series of asses. (S)

(1989): Surprise, attack, understate, or overstate, but whatever you do, avoid the two cardinal sins of being either boring or predictable. (WS)

(1995): I like big changes, it's what make you react differently. I'm not the kind of guy that goes from one blues group to another blues group. It helps you through exercising choice with all of these people, to try and figure out what it is precisely that you have to offer. I'm trying to whittle down what it is that I do, to find the essence of it. So that you hope to cut away all the stuff that is not really you, all of the deadwood, faking, copying, and ripping off.

Self-imposed pressure is the only way I know how to get through life. Taking things that are a little beyond me, but not so much beyond me that I'll fail. The trick is to try to play, as a drummer, music where you don't completely understand what is happening. You understand seventy percent of it, but you don't understand why thirty percent occurs or is like that. Then you have something that you're reaching for. You learn from that and then you go and do the next project. (TMI)

(1982): I like to feel I know what is going on in the other instruments, that I could probably play the parts the other musicians have and know how the music fits together. I think this helps you in designing the drum part for the piece in question. . . .

It looks to me when I see myself drumming always as though I'm only just holding on to the drumsticks. It looks like a very light grip and in fact it is. I think in particular my left stick . . . I picked it up wrong when I was a kid and stayed with a bad habit. What happened then was I started playing with musicians who played electric instruments and there were no microphones on the drums. I couldn't make my main beat with my left stick heard very clearly, so instinctively I started to get the higher frequencies out of the snare drum; which you do by getting a rim shot. So mostly I play because of that fault off the rim of the drum for the louder strokes, which gives me a fairly individual snare drum sound.

Sometimes in tunes I think the drummer is and will want to be simple and complex at the same time. So that if there is an odd-numbered rhythm pattern, perhaps 17 or some trickier beat like that, which half of the orchestra has, it may be best to offset that with a 4/4 pulse. So the audience locates the dance groove in it, locates the simple, essential beat, from which it then perceives the tension of the odd number on top. If you merely present the odd number against nothing, there is no tension and no excitement. The excitement comes from the tension and release. (BB)

chris (1994): Initially any band is only as active and creative and as good as its drummer. That's where it all starts and he was very much a driving force in that period. That influence on Yes was a very good one. Bill was a particularly good influence on me. (ITS)

peter (1994): He's probably the best drummer I've ever played with, but he has a tendency to be very pompous and he's always had that. Everybody else in Yes would take drugs except for Bill. Bill was always the straight man, he would smirk and look at us being kind of stupid, because we were out of our heads. Bill was always the restraining influence. He was always democratic, sensible, and very tight with money. I used to list every gig that we did; Bill not only listed the gigs, but also how much money we were paid. So there's the difference, you see. I used to put down what the audience response was, how well we went down, and Bill would write down how much money we made. If anyone wanted to borrow any money, it was usually me or Jon who was borrowing money off of Bill, Bill would write it down in a little book. Bill was always like that. . . . He was very much a jazz snob and he really regarded rock 'n' roll as something to just pass the time of day. He certainly turned me on to a lot of jazz music and conversely I turned him on to a few things that he hadn't heard. He was into Art Blakey and people like Jack DeJohnette. We would listen to John McLaughlin and Coltrane and that kind of stuff. (TMI)

eddie (1995): Bill was the only guy in the band who didn't do drugs or drink, really. He had a great sense of humor—he was a funny guy. He had great timing, he was incredible. He has that pseudo-English intellectuality about him too. (TMI)

tony (1985): When Bill joined Yes, he was a total jazzer, from the heart. (K)

rick (1975): He has absolute precision and the sense of someone taking a real care over the tonal quality you can get out of a drum set. (CM)

trevor rabin (1995): On the Union tour Bill and I got on very well. We used to jam before shows and I loved playing with him. He's just incredible.

Bill has no pretenses and no ego. He's purely a musician. The amount of integrity that Bill Bruford has as a person and as a musician is more than I think the entire band has put together. He's an amazing, wonderful guy. You can only take your hat off to a guy who leaves on the brink of their biggest album! (TMI)

steve (1982): Bill's mainly distinctive thing was the old Bruford snare drum, which used to be the studio engineers' nightmare, "Agh! How do you do that?" But he always got it through, especially with Eddie in the early days. He's not a greedy musician, you know? When we were mixing, he was into his own dimension. When I look back sometimes his drums are quite quiet and yet they still have effect. (BB)

(1993): Bill says, "I just hit drums and that's all, bang, bang, bang." And of course that disguises his other more complicated side that he can't always deal with, can't always talk about, how he writes all these songs, all these tunes. It's not often a drummer does that, not many drummers write as much kind of musical ideas as Bill. He's very creative. (NFTE)

(1994): Bill's classic statement before a Yes show was, "Okay, I'm going to play everything different tonight! See ya!" It was exactly that, all of the drum breaks . . . he'd do something else there. Don't rely on him; if you're not sure, count! And you had to because sometimes we'd come to a drum break, which we had loads of in songs, and Bill would really cut a new direction. And when he did that it could be really sideways. (TMI)

bill (1994): That's true and I know that made me no friends. But that was my improvising nature. I wanted to not play the same thing, for my own sanity I had to try to look at the music fresh every night. I still do, actually. But now I have a greater repertoire to call on and a better technical ability, so I don't make such a mess of it. But it's true, I'm sure, that I was an extremely irritating person to work with on many occasions. But that would be one aspect of my personality that I hope I would have changed. (TMI)

ON TONY KAYE

Tony Kaye is known as the "Gentleman of Rock" for his polite demeanor and his distinguished looks. He is not a flashy or flamboyant player, but a supporting team member of the band. After Tony left Yes, he went on to form his own group, Badger, with David Foster (who had been a member of Jon Anderson's first group, the Warriors). When Badger folded, he played with the bands Detective and Badfinger before rejoining Yes for its amazing comeback in the 1980s.

tony (1988): Long, improvised organ solos . . . I certainly don't want to hear it. And I certainly don't want to hear long drum improvisations or long guitar improvisations, for that matter. (MAT)

(1985): My secret ambition has always been to play the piano with the Rolling Stones. (K)

(1988): I'm not a writer. I'm not a singer, and I'm not a lyricist. I'm a musician . . . I'm just an instrumentalist, really. (MAT)

steve (1982): Tony Kaye was not what you'd call an up-front keyboard player; he was a good group member, he was always participating and contributing. (R)

peter (1994): He and I played together very easily. We never had to discuss anything. Often with Chris and Bill I had to discuss things, but with Tony and I there was never any problem. And he was good at filling in gaps; if there was a gap he would fill it in. He wasn't a great guy for picking out riffs. . . . Tony would fill in the hole underneath. Often he and I wouldn't know what we were playing, we wouldn't even know what the chords were. They just sounded right and that was okay. It was very natural. (TMI)

alan (1994): I never got to know Tony until we did *90125* and then we spent a lot of time together and became very good friends. (TMI)

geoff (1980): I think what interested Chris Squire in my approach to playing keyboards was that it was more in keeping with the way Tony Kaye played. I've always admired Kaye's playing. I like that sort of Hammond organ sound he used to get. (K)

eddie (1995): He's probably one of the greatest B-3 players around. The reason he left the band was because everyone wanted him to get into synthesizers and Mellotrons and stuff and he was so happy hammering away on the B-3. (TMI)

trevor rabin (1995): Tony has his own kind of style. He kind of fits himself into the background, he has self-imposed limitations. (TMI)

ON STEVE HOWE

When people talk of Steve Howe, the word "virtuoso" is almost always used. He is clearly one of the finest guitarists walking the planet today (as testified by his peers—he was voted Best Overall Guitarist by the readers of *Guitar Player* magazine five years in a row and inducted into their hall of fame). He is equally at home playing a Japanese koto as he is working a pedal steel guitar (as well as other numerous instruments). After Yes fell apart in 1981, Steve has kept busy working with Asia, GTR, and other solo and collaborative projects.

steve (1994): There was something Paul [McCartney] said in the movie *Let It Be* that I took as a little bit of a derogatory statement towards George Harrison, which I didn't like. But what he said was, "A guitarist has got to have riffs! If George doesn't have any riffs, we're in trouble." I've always believed that's true and I've always got riffs. (TMI)

(1993): When I was in Yes, I really tried to avoid clichés. Every time I would start to play some sort of conventional guitar riff, I'd think, "That's not what I'm going to play. I've got to find something else here." I'm not as committed to being avant-garde these days, because playing something more conventional can be good under the right circumstances. But I still try to keep it to a minimum. (GW)

ON BECOMING A VEGETARIAN

steve (1992): Traveling and performing caused me to think more about what I was eating. For a long time, something bothered me about eating meat, although I couldn't quite place it. Then, while traveling in America, having dinner one night, and having this chicken placed in front of me—it was typically overcooked, greasy, you know, probably micro-

Steve enjoying one of his many hobbies, with Philadelphia DJ Ed Sciaky.

At an Asia end-of-tour party, he takes off his mask to honor a request for the Beatles.

waved—I just right there made this decision not to eat it and I felt good about the decision. It stuck with me. [My wife and I] became interested in classes offered at the East West Center like reflexology and psychosynthesis. I began going for treatments. We were really getting going. And we gave up the idea of "take-away" instant solutions to health. (MT)

steve (1982): [on the issue of privacy for a media figure] I was talking to some Japanese people and they said, "We heard you meditate," and I said, "Who told you?" They said, "So and so said you like this peace and quiet before the shows." And although at first I was sort of offended, because a bit of my private life had escaped into the media, which it is now by me repeating it, but there's a cutoff point. They were asking me, "What is it? What's it all about?" And all I said was that it's what I've found. That was my way of keeping my privacy about what I do. You know, I could really start preaching, saying, "Why don't you run down the street, call this number toll-free, and learn this technique? . . ." I don't want to do that. (VT)

jon (1994): When Steve Howe joined the group it made us more musical. Our scope was more musical. When Steve came in we had all of this baroque attitude to music, and this classical trained attitude to music. Steve could really jump from one thing to another very fast, a very talented man. Me and Steve became very close. We had very similar attitudes to making music, so we'd sit down and write songs without any effort. (ITS)

tony (1994): I was probably one of the first people in the band to have heard Steve. He was playing in a club I used to frequent in a band called Bodast. It wasn't that progressive, it was mainly a rock 'n' roll band. I saw Steve play and I thought this guy has really got something else. But he was playing in a band that was really kind of a raunchy rock 'n' roll band, which is something I kind of wanted for the band at that time. As soon as he came into the band he went into a different mode and started playing much more progressive guitar than this sort of raunchy player that I remembered. (ITS)

bill (1995): He changed the band when he came in. I take guitarists for granted, but I don't think I should take Steve for granted, he's really good. Certainly the stuff he did when I was in the band with him I thought was really effective and it's stood the test of time. They are very whistle-able solos, very sing-able and very melodically astute. He was very good.

When we rerecorded some of that music [for the *Symphonic Music of Yes*] Steve would be trying other ideas for a solo passage like on "I've Seen All Good People," the shuffle one. It was like he was playing the wrong song. Everybody would say, "No, Steve, play the right song." What they meant was play exactly the same solo, because all of us have become so attached to those guitar solos that he did, that to change them is practically impossible. They have become part of the tune. (TMI)

rick (1985): Steve is such an extremely talented guitarist . . . and I'll probably get shot for saying this . . . I think Steve's guitar playing was too good for Asia. . . . He's such a stunning, tremendous player. (TR)

alan (1994): Steve and myself were really good friends in the early days. We used to spend a lot of time talking in each other's rooms and listening to music and things like that. (TMI)

trevor horn (1980): Steve is one of the straightest, fairest, nicest people you could wish to meet. I take Steve as an example for a lot of things that I do, because he is so together. (R)

geoff (1994): I always have got a lot of time for Steve, particularly because we always got on very well even though we're very, very different types of people, but we still have a good mutual respect for each other. It's not that easy when you have a keyboard player working with a guitarist.

What I liked about him was that he was prepared to try anything out. He's not one of those guitarists who says, "That's my sound, therefore that's the way it is." He's got all of these weird and wonderful guitars that he tries to get the most out of. I think that is really what separates him as an individual, he's a classic guitarist above even people like Trevor Rabin—who I would not consider to be that type of guitarist. He doesn't do that full sort of experimentation. Steve will have slide guitars . . . he even brought in a hurdy-gurdy one day! He's pretty crazy, but it's the way that he is and the way Yes was when he was the guitarist.

Steve, I always associate in my mind as being the Yes guitarist, but he's really not been a fundamental member of the group for fifteen years nearly. You can look at the ABWH offshoot and the Union tour and album, but really he's not been the guitarist of Yes for fifteen years and yet my perception of him is that he is. (TMI)

eddie (1995): Steve always reminded me of a racehorse: If you said "Boo" to him he'd probably jump! He lived in an isolated, peaceful kind of thing—he'd like to get down and stuff, but he was nervous about extraneous things . . . it's hard to explain. What a phenomenal guitarist! (TMI)

patrick (1995): Steve was . . . extremely meticulous about the way he wanted this music to be performed, even if it didn't make any sense! He is very talented, hardworking also, lots of ideas, lovely imagination, and he has lots of guitars. He has so many guitars! During the show I would say, "Why did you change guitars? It sounds exactly the same as the last one!" Some nights there was so much echo on the stage we were playing that you couldn't hear the difference anyway. It's like doing some figure skating or whatever, it's part of the show. It becomes almost a prop at this time. . . . Steve was very sexy. I like ladies, but I am not afraid to say that I thought Steve was very sexy on stage at the time. He was like a stage animal. He had a fantastic stage presence. (TMI)

chris (1994): Steve is still the same. He is still in guitar world. He's like, "*Oh!* Are there other people playing?" (YV)

trevor rabin (1995): Steve was such an integral part of Yes. Before doing the Union tour I really didn't understand how important Steve was to

Rick Wakeman in full period regalia.
ROBERT ELLIS/REPFOTO

the actual writing process of the band, besides the guitar playing. He was a major part of the writing. (TMI)

ON RICK WAKEMAN

Rick Wakeman is one of the most popular and identifiable artists to come out of the progressive rock scene. He is known not only for his considerable musical talents, but also for his flamboyant and extravagant stage productions and the infamous Wakeman sense of humor. He has easily been the most busy and prolific Yes member, with literally countless sessions and albums to his credit.

bill (1994): He could play all kinds of countermelodies and other figures and had different ways of harmonizing things. He could modulate without you noticing it. He could do all the tricks that an academy guy could do. So suddenly the joins of music didn't seem so bad. You'd go from letter A to letter B and there'd be this horrible scrunch before. He could smooth the thing over. . . . That was a huge leap forward.

(1995): He could make a silk purse out of a sow's ear. He had the magic. Rick knew so much and Jon knew so little; now, I'm talking about mechanics, not emotions or feelings—they were even on that. Jon could sing the most awful three-note dirge over and over, but of course Rick could extend it. He could reharmonize it, make it change key without anyone being able to detect where the modulation was. Even Jon wouldn't know that it had modulated! He could play it in the style of Rachminoff . . . it was like, "Rick, stop a minute. Let's just have ideas one, five, and seven."

If the only thing he'd done was the solo in "Roundabout," that alone was worth its weight in gold. That was a tremendous bit, a wailing solo without a note of jazz in it. There's no phrasing in it, no breathing like a jazz player would. That's a characteristic of it and I'm not denigrating it—it was great! It sounded different. It didn't sound like the Allman Brothers. This thing steamed, and playing that with him every night was a groove, because it just flew along! (TMI)

jon (1994): [about Rick's wild lifestyle] He was early grunge. (S)

alan (1994): Rick is completely nuts. He's out there having fun . . . he's pretty much a crazy guy at heart and he still likes making his life full of being Rick. (TMI)

chris (1994): [on the Union tour] I honestly didn't think I was going to get on with Rick, because I could never quite grasp his sense of humor in the past. Trevor Rabin once asked me what he was like and I said, "Well, if he says 'Good Morning,' you know he's telling a lie!" However, as it turned out the pleasant surprise was that it was completely the opposite. He was very sweet and we had a very good time together. (YV)

trevor rabin (1995): Rick is just so incredible. I was really a legitimate Rick Wakeman fan before I joined Yes. I always found him to be one of the magnetizing factors in the band. Rick is such a huge, integral part of the nucleus of Yes. He is the most recognizable personality from the group and I believe as a solo artist he has sold more records than Yes! (TMI)

geoff (1994): I suppose people would say the classic keyboardist for Yes would be Rick Wakeman, but it's a bit more diverse than that because the really early Yes period was quite happily Tony Kaye. Then you've got Patrick and myself, who did one album with the band. So it's a strange sort of thing. (TMI)

trevor rabin (1994): I loved working with Rick [on the Union tour]. Rick and I got on tremendously well, musically and personally. I got on with everyone else, but Rick in particular was a good moment for me. (YM)

tony (1971): I admire organists like Rick Wakeman and Keith Emerson, but I'm not into the technique thing and my job is to work together with Yes. [This was six months before Wakeman replaced Kaye in Yes!] (MM)

eddie (1995): He was into Benny Hill, that sort of hanging-out-in-the-pub type humor. And the rest of the band was into Monty Python—a bit more dopey or something. He was kind of an outsider, but he did his parts really well. He's just a really accomplished player. (TMI)

Alan White is perhaps the unsung hero of Yes. He is not only the spectacular drummer who has anchored the group musically for over twenty years, but also a major composer to some of Yes's best-loved works. Alan is known by his fans and everyone in the music business as truly one of the nicest and most easygoing individuals you could possibly meet, which in the band's volatile chemistry is another important contribution!

alan (1995): It's not enough to be a good drummer. To be a great drummer, you have to analyze the musicians around you, that are playing with you, and use it to develop the music. Have your ears open, don't listen to what you are doing alone, because what people are going to hear is the whole piece. Don't try to be an extrovert, because drummers tend to do that sometimes. They'll be playing their thing and they forget about the music around them. All of that technique is adaptable to the music, you just need to use it within the framework of the song. Be selective about what you play, find where it is necessary. (TMI)

(1994): They won't let me sing anymore. I used to in the old days. They used to call me "Astro White," because I used to sing the very high harmonies that were even above Jon sometimes—in falsetto. (YV)

I'm a pretty good cook. It's like a hobby of mine, I find it to be a form of relaxation. I cook all the time, my wife loves it! I think it's kind of therapeutic in a way, I just enjoy cooking. (TMI)

trevor horn (1980): I thought Alan was the best drummer I'd ever heard. He was just the best. And being a producer, I'd worked with all sorts of drummers. But eventually meeting Alan was the first time I'd ever, ever met the perfect drummer. (R)

rick (1973): I like Alan, he's a great guy to work with, and he's a nice person as well. The only thing I can say about him is that he's changed the band in a strange way. You either like him or you don't. In America it's been an extreme thing, people either like the way the music has gone or they don't. It's very clear-cut. (MM)

trevor rabin (1995): Alan is the sweetest guy in the world. We're great friends. Anyone who says anything bad about Alan is lying! I've heard the most terrible things about Jon and Chris and I'm sure they've heard terrible things about me—some of which are misunderstandings or things that are hopefully not true. But there's no such thing as a bad word about Alan. It's almost aggravating—that is about the only bad thing about him!

He's a tremendous musician. He approaches drumming like a keyboard player, he plays the piano, but then so do lots of drummers. Phil Collins plays the piano, but he plays like a drummer—like a great drummer! Alan thinks like a keyboard player, he thinks of the whole arrangement when he's playing. He tried to keep away from doing normal things, which I love about him. And he's very quick to pick up that this part goes from 7/4 to 9/8 and he gets it straightaway. You don't have to wait for him to figure it out; he's a very clever player. (TMI)

patrick (1995): Alan was action man. He was always action man and he will always be action man. He is very energetic and a great drummer. Always positive, I've never seen him negative. He's never said anything bad about anybody. He was always great to work with, always understanding, hardworking, a gentle man. Drummers are usually moody, they have mood swings . . . but Alan was always on time, prompt, a great guy. He was a great bud, not really a friend, but a good acquaintance. (TMI)

geoff (1994): I remember Alan White used to say to me when I was in the group that he had been in the band for about eight years and people always said Bruford was the drummer and probably still do today. It must be quite difficult for the new guy to come in and really have to carry that mantle. (TMI)

bill (1978): Alan plays very differently from me; he is good at steaming on all four. Very good timekeeper. Maybe he didn't do the fancy bits I did, but we are radically different and I think when Alan came it was a change. I think that now he has worked his own style into the group. (TP)

ON PATRICK MORAZ

Patrick Moraz is a man of kinetic energy. He has an intensity and passion for life and music that spills over into everything he does. He is also a virtuoso keyboardist of the highest order. Since he left Yes in 1976, Patrick has pursued a number of solo and collaborative projects and was the keyboardist for the Moody Blues for a number of years.

patrick (1995): I think virtuosity is an objective, but it's not my aim to be considered a virtuoso. It goes much deeper than virtuosity. It's the essential emotionality or the emotional essentially. (TMI)

alan (1994): Patrick was also crazy! He's just a wild guy. I knew him pretty well, but he's the kind of person who you really couldn't get to know in depth, I don't think. (TMI)

jon (1975): [He has] a frenetic kind of poetry, a schizoid intenseness. A very intense person is Patrick, and he wants to say everything now or yesterday. (MM)

chris (1991): He's a strange one in the first place, because he's a Swiss rock musician. How many are there? How many famous Swiss rock bands are there? Not too many! They probably play very well in time. (YY)

steve (1994): Patrick was willing to take on a tremendous amount and we had to bend a bit, because he wasn't really like Rick. He didn't play like Rick, although he could provide the same double-handed keyboard style. He was quite a different animal. It's a shame he wasn't given time to mature, but fortunately for us Rick came back when things weren't going well with Patrick, between Patrick and us. It was a time of clinging on to the raft for your life, because Yes was an unpredictable sort of thing at this time. (TMI)

bill (1995): He always had in this biography of himself that he'd won this Zurich jazz piano competition when he was twenty years old. And I sensed that underneath there was a jazz player ready to get out. Chick Corea had written a song for him and there was jazz pianist in there at one time, much more than Rick Wakeman, who hasn't got a note of jazz in him. He's entirely classical, he doesn't know what a blue note is! Which is fine, it's a phenomenally European thing. He plays lots of arpeggios with almost no syncopation. Diatonic stuff. You couldn't pay an American to play that. He wouldn't know how to, he'd have to hit a blue note. But Moraz had a fair amount of jazz in him. (TMI)

ON GEOFF DOWNES

After leaving Yes in 1981, Geoff Downes became one of the founding members of the supergroup Asia with Steve Howe, Carl Palmer, and John Wetton. They experienced huge success, but unfortunately equally huge personnel problems. When Asia went on hiatus, Geoff went on to release a solo album and do some production work (notably Steve Howe's GTR project). The late 1980s found Asia reforming, with Geoff's strong keyboard textures and songwriting an integral part of it.

geoff (1980): I've always considered the keyboards to be a part of the rhythm section. They sit more with the bass and drums, but you can also spend your time weaving melodies. I don't like the idea of playing chords all night. Playing keyboards with a band should be a combination of playing chords and melodies so the lines you play are more like arrangements than they are a frantic solo. I think Yes had been getting into too much of that kind of thing. Their music was getting to sound like everyone soloing all at once. Now, the overall arrangement gets more thought than it had been getting. (K)
(1994): I like to read. I like to do crosswords. I like to go snow skiing when I can. I like to go mountain biking, anything to just get away and clear my head. Music has always fascinated me and still continues to fascinate me. Having been in it for twenty-odd years, I still haven't lost the excitement, or the drive or the adrenaline. I don't think so anyway. That's what really keeps you going and that was one of the reasons why I felt that we [Asia] had to get the music together again. I had really missed the live stuff, going out on the road and playing gigs. (MNN)

chris (1980): Geoff Downes is the best keyboard player Yes have ever had. He listens. (YAB)

alan (1994): I never became that close to Geoff Downes, but I did after a while. Probably after he wasn't in the band, more than when he was in the band, to tell you the truth. I kept meeting him in different circumstances after he was in Asia, and got to know him a little better. (TMI)

ON TREVOR HORN

Trevor Horn is one of most successful record producers working in the music business today. Some of the many artists he has worked with include Paul

McCartney, Art of Noise, Frankie Goes to Hollywood, Rod Stewart, and Seal. The unfortunate side of this is that we don't get the chance to hear him as a performing artist any longer. His last major release was *Adventures in Modern Recording,* which came out 1981. His place in Yes's history is assured, however, with the excellent work he did on *Drama, 90125,* and *Big Generator.*

trevor horn (1980): I don't honestly know whether I could ever sing the old songs as well as Jon Anderson can. I know that because he wrote them. He wrote them for him.

When it came to writing lyrics for Yes it was like a relief because I didn't have to write smarty-pants things [as in the Buggles]. I could write more the sort of things that I like. (R)

trevor rabin (1985): I loved what he did with the Buggles and I thought what he did on *Drama* was very good. He had a tough job filling Jon Anderson's shoes on stage. It's much easier filling a musician's spot than the front man's . . . the lead guy. It's very difficult. He had a lot of guts to do what he did. (R)

eddie (1995): Poor Trevor, poor guy. I didn't go on the tours, but I heard they were throwing things at him and stuff. (TMI)

alan (1994): He's not a person who is easy to get close to. He comes from the same part of England that I do and I think he's very talented and he knows what he wants to hear. He uses that talent and is a great producer. (TMI)

geoff (1994): I'd worked with Trevor a long time before [I was in Yes]. We had a good working relationship. I think we both understood each other. We were both guys from the north of England who had come down to London to make a living in the music scene. There was a sort of parity between us. There was the two of us and we struggled very hard. The Buggles thing was a big challenge for us, really, to come up from being complete nobodies and our first record is the number-one record around the world. There was a lot of enjoyment in that. We had a very good understanding between us as a working team throughout Yes and a good respect for each other. (TMI)

patrick (1995): He is a very good producer and an extremely shrewd businessman and so on. He knew what he was doing. (TMI)

ON TREVOR RABIN

Trevor Rabin is the catalyst behind Yes's enormous success in the 1980s. His excellent guitar playing, singing, and songwriting have been featured prominently on the last four Yes releases, to the delight of new and old fans. When he is not working with Yes, he participates in many musical collaborations and has released several fine solo albums over the years.

trevor rabin (1984): One thing I never wanted to do was just get on stage and play Steve Howe licks. I have a Gibson 175 at home, but I certainly wasn't going to go on the road with the Steve Howe guitar. I was going to change the guitar arrangements and put my style into it. Otherwise there would be no point. I'm not interested in filling someone's shoes. And the great thing was that the rest of the band was really into it and said, "You can change what you like." (BAM)

(1995): While I'd liked the Yes stuff I'd heard, I wasn't someone who had bought every Yes album before I'd joined. I had three Yes albums when I was growing up, *Time and a Word,* which I loved. Then I loved *Fragile* and *The Six Wives Of Henry VIII.* Those were the three albums from the Yes camp that I had and just loved them. But beyond that I really didn't know much about the band. So when it came to rehearsing things like "And You and I," I wasn't too aware of it. It's one thing learning it, that's the easy part—there's nothing technically challenging. The difficult part is trying to make it your own. It took some time for me to feel a part of Yes and what Yes is.

I appreciated that I was given the time of day by the Yes fans, I was never booed off stage or anything like that. And I had heard about what some fans did with Trevor Horn. At our first show ever, I was absolutely terrified. I didn't know what to expect—if I was going to be pounded with bottles or what was going to happen, because Steve was such an integral part of the lineup that had preceded me. I thought, "I'm not just a replacement guitarist that has been hired, I'm a guy that has somewhat been a catalyst in the new band. I joined this band and suddenly it became Yes and I'm going to be blamed for ruining the band!" So I feel there was a lot more patience dealing with me from real diehard fans and even the people who still feel that I shouldn't be in Yes are gracious and polite to me. (TMI)

(1987): Chris is pretty trusting; he just lets me get on with it. He knows that when I come up with something, there is always thought behind it. I never just do something—throw this on, throw that on—I always have an idea. (GW)

(1995): It's funny, but a lot of the stuff I do no one hears and my function in the [Yes] team if you like, from a record company's point of view, is, "Oh, he writes the hits." And I hate that, it really bugs the shit out of me. It's like an artist doing a painting, he doesn't hide it in his closet, he wants people to see it. And I'd like people to hear [my unreleased] stuff and it's lying in the basement. This kind of music isn't fashion-oriented or what the radio demographic format is now . . . it doesn't really adhere to any of that stuff.

(1994): One of the things that multi-instrumentalists suffer from is a lack of identity. Todd Rundgren is a great guitar player, he's a great drummer. But he's never really been known in the guitar world as a great guitar player. It's definitely my first instrument, the first thing I gravitate towards is the guitar if I am going to be soloist or performer. But if I'm orchestrating and doing that side of things, I go to the piano.

(1995): I'm certainly not the biggest fan of what I do. I'm very critical and whenever I finish anything, whether it is with Yes or a solo project, I never like it afterwards. I always say, "God, it could have been so much better!" I never listen to anything and say, "That's perfect." (TMI)

(1987): I'm pretty boring. I write and work out. I have weights at home, I swim for a half hour each day, then bicycle for about an hour; so I do about two hours of workout a day. Years ago, I went through this silly sort of thing, thinking that holding the weights was going to affect my hands. That was a stupid concern. (GW)

alan (1991): Trevor has a vast amount of talent and a vast array of music that not only appeals to the new fans, but to the old fans as well. I think we've only begun to tap the energy this guy has. (WS)

(1994): Trevor is a great friend of mine. We get along really well. I've got to know him over the last twelve years and he is a very, very, very talented musician. And I respect his musicianship and friendship greatly. (TMI)

steve (1984): I've played with Trevor Rabin, so I know what he's like. He is highly musical and he's very quick. I mean, not only fast, but quick to pick up new ideas. (R)

rick (1991): I have a stunning respect for Trevor Rabin. We've become bosom pals. For a lot of the stuff that he did in the eighties, he said, "Fancy a journey into the past?" "Love to!" I said. And he said, "Imagine that you were in the band with me then. Here's the music. What would you do with it?" (K)

trevor horn (1985): He made much more of a difference to Yes than Geoff and I ever did as members of the band. Not just because of his playing on guitar and keyboards and his singing, even though all are extraordinary, but because he has this naive stubbornness that's a strength. (MN)

tony (1985): Trevor is one of the most talented people I've ever met. His musical background is impeccable, and he is such an emotional gutsy player, a great guitarist. (K)

patrick (1995): I love Trevor's musicianship and personality. He's a great guy and so on, but he's not Steve. (TMI)

bill (1994): I think Trevor Rabin is enormously talented, but I'm not sure somehow that talent alone can give you a band's heart and soul. I don't think it can. I think no matter how talented you are, he's still an outsider to Yes. (TMI)

eddie (1995): I have a lot of respect for him and he's done some great things with Yes. But I think one of the problems he's had is that he shouldn't be producing the band. I think he tends to sterilize Yes a little bit. He'll do things like record Alan drumming and then he'll replace everything Alan did with samples. And then he'll move them around till he thinks they're more in time or something. It becomes a bit more precise, but it loses the beauty of the whole thing. (TMI)

geoff (1994): I think Trevor Rabin is a very, very accomplished musician, as I think most musicians in Yes have been. I think they must have had something. (TMI)

THE QUESTIONS

As I interviewed the band for this book, I came up with two questions that I decided to ask each member. I thought it might be interesting to see if there was a song or album that represented what Yes was about to them and also what their desert island discs would be. I was not disappointed with their answers.

IS THERE A SONG OR LP THAT SUMS UP YES FOR YOU?

peter: No, not really. It's not a part of my listening list anymore. I like the new album *Talk* and I liked *90125*. I thought that was terrific, I like Trevor Horn's work a lot. It was as much Trevor Horn as the band, really. I think Trevor Rabin did excellent work on *Talk* as well.

alan: It's so hard to answer that question because it spans such an era and certain songs relate to those eras. I think "Awaken" is a great song to pick for that mid-seventies to late seventies era. I think "Starship Trooper" is great for the prior era as an image of what the band was. I think if you want to go into *Topographic*, side three and "Ritual" are great pieces of music. They are very adventurous.

Each album was a definite new kind of direction for each period of the band. There was always a number on the album that meant more about that period than others and most of them are the longer pieces on the albums. We got into them and developed them more and they were a statement of where the band was at that time. For instance I feel that "Endless Dream" would be that sort of song for the current lineup of Yes.

bill: Definitely *Close to the Edge*. That has "Siberian Khatru," which I thought was really hip too. I like that one. We rehearsed that one up for ABWH, but we never used it. It was really very steamy and you could play it with all the authority now that we really didn't have then. So it would have sounded at least twice as good. But definitely *Close to the Edge* is the thing. The single of "Roundabout" was good, but it sounds a bit tired now, doesn't it? Rick Wakeman's organ solo on that was tremendous fun, there's no doubt about it. We were all wailing on that.

geoff: Well, I think really it's some of the earlier stuff. "And You and I," "Starship Trooper," and "Yours Is No Disgrace" . . . they summed up really what we were going for in "Machine Messiah." That was really the type of music that incorporated up sections, performance sections, vocals . . . a complete mixture, a bit of an epic. Those are the tracks for me that really sum up what Yes is about.

patrick: When I saw the show live in 1991, with the Union tour, I thought "Awaken" was the greatest piece of the show. I feel closer to that piece than "Gates of Delirium." "Gates" was more a collage of different little melodies put together; that's the way Jon worked. Although *Topographic Oceans* has been denigrated by critics, I think it came to life when we played it. . . . If we could do it now with the technology it would be incredible.

steve: At the moment I'd say "To Be Over," because that's the one that bowled me over the most [recently]. . . . There's no way you could look at it and say, "This is just a song." It's a quarter of an album, it's got an array of different areas that it works within, and has one of the most powerful middle eights that Jon and I ever collaborated on, to me. That's part of the reason I want to do it, because "After all your soul will still surrender . . ." is one of those powerful things. I wrote those chords and I had that melody and I think I had "After all," and that's all I had. I didn't know what to say after that. But I knew I had something that was tight there and Jon elaborated on it. For me that's the high point of *Relayer*. That is thoroughbred Yes.

chris: "Heart of the Sunrise" has always felt that way to me.

trevor rabin: There's so many different parts of Yes. "Sweet Dreams" with Tony Kaye and Peter Banks is a highlight for me; *Fragile* is another highlight of Yes and *90125* as well. *Talk* is probably the most successful album musically the band has done. That is the album for me; I'm very happy with it.

eddie: This might sound stupid, but I liked "Time and a Word," I really liked that song. I don't think it was done justice on that record, but it's a beautiful song. Another song I do like is "And You and I." There's something really great about that song.

rick (1992): Pieces like "And You and I" and "Close to the Edge" were bigger than the band, they were more important than the band or any individual. They were more powerful than the band. There are certain pieces of Yes music that are in control of you, rather than you being in control of it, and "And You and I" is undoubtedly one of them. "Close to the Edge," for me, is another, and "Awaken" is another, so it is amazing to have two such pieces on one album [*Close to the Edge*]. (ITS)

jon (1991): We did what I think is the best Yes piece of music, called "Awaken" [on *Going for the One*]. It's a beautiful piece of music in structure and form, and it's got everything that I would desire of a group of musicians in this life. (YY)

WHAT ARE YOUR DESERT ISLAND DISCS?

alan: I'd take some classical stuff. I like Ravel and Sibelius. I like a lot of different people for different reasons. I like Ravel's *Daphnis et Chole*, that's my morning music when I'm waking up. I'd take some Vangelis stuff . . . *Opera Sauvage*, which is one of my favorite Vangelis albums. There's a lot of jazz things I like. I play the Yellowjackets a lot. I like Sting. I recently got this record called *Music from Around the World* and I've been obsessed with it recently. There's a lot of stuff from Africa and things like that. I listen to Soundgarden, I've got their new album and I like some of it. There's reams of stuff, really; if it's good I like it.

peter: This is not definitive. I tried to put down albums that have influenced me, not necessarily ones I would listen to, but kind of classic albums that had an effect on my playing or on me personally.

1. *Rain Tree Crow*, which is by Rain Tree Crow, which is basically the group Japan. They reformed and did what I think is a terrific album, which everyone else hated.
2. Pat Metheny, probably his last one, *Secret Stories*, or another album I liked a lot was *Offramp*.
3. A guy named Claus Ogerman, a German arranger, did an album called *City Scapes*. That's got Michael Brecker on tenor sax on that one.
4. Bill Evans, an album called *Symbiois*, which was also done with Claus Ogerman.
5. Benjamin Britten, the composer, I don't really have a favorite version of this, but any album with his string quartets.
6. Talking Heads, *Remain in Light*.
7. Frankie Goes to Hollywood, *Welcome to the Pleasure Dome*, purely for the production, which I think is terrific.
8. Miles Davis, either *Sketches of Spain* or *Kind of Blue*, I'm kind of torn there.

9. Weather Report has a live album called *8:30* which I love for Jaco Pastorius's bass playing. I think it's marvelous.
10. Another album I used to love and play to death—I literally wore this album out—was by the Soft Machine and it was called *Third*.
11. Cheating here, there's a James Brown box set. I can't put down just one James Brown album.
12. Another box set, Keith Jarrett, *The Sun Bear Concerts*.
13. John Coltrane, *A Love Supreme*, which is one of my favorites.
14. Pete Townshend's *Empty Glass*.
15. Ralph Vaughan Williams, any albums with his symphonies number five and six on them. He was a terrific composer, not particularly avant-garde for his time, he was pretty conservative.
16. Airto did a great album called *I'm Fine, How Are You?* which came out in the mid-seventies.
17. I wanted to choose a Joni Mitchell album, but I couldn't decide which one to put down, it would probably be *For the Roses* or *Don Juan's Reckless Daughter*, which I also like for Jaco's bass playing.
18. I would also include the Ravel piano concerto done by Pascal Roge, who is a terrific French pianist with the Montreal Symphony Orchestra.
19. There's album by David Sancious who wrote a wonderful record called *True Stories* [produced by Eddie Offord]. It's a bit of an obscure one. I was just listening to it the other night and I remembered that I was nuts about it when it came out.
20. King Crimson, *Discipline*.

bill: Oh that's really hard! I'd definitely have to have *My Song* by Keith Jarrett. I'd definitely have to have *Bitches Brew* by Miles. I don't think there's any rock album at all that I have to have. I can't think of any rock record that has shaken me to the bones, maybe Lennon's *Walls and Bridges*, the first King Crimson album, and *Close to the Edge*. I'd like to have *Close to the Edge* as a memory of a very good time with that band. *Adagio*, Albinoni's thing *Adagio for Strings*. Very funereal, but I have to have that. A few English hymns. I don't know, that's about it, really. Without being given more time to think about it . . . we've all heard so much music and there's probably lots of other things I could think of.

geoff: I'd certainly take some Eagles stuff; I love the Eagles. I'd take some Abba stuff as well. Supertramp, I mean this is all stuff from the seventies and early eighties. A lot of the stuff in the eighties doesn't really inspire me. I'd take some Journey, if only for Steve Perry's singing, and I'd take some Paul Rodgers for his vocals. Probably some of his solo stuff as opposed to the Bad Company records. That would be a sort of a fair kickoff selection, I think.

patrick: I would take the *Suite in B minor* by Bach and the *48 Preludes and Fugue* as performed by Keith Jarrett. I would take all of Keith Jarrett's work, at least his *Paris Concert* or the *Bremen Lausanne Concert* or any piano concert, even the Vienna one. I am an unconditional fan of his music. I would probably take *Relayer* as a souvenir and I would take *Long Distance Voyager* as a souvenir. I wouldn't need to take my solo albums. They sound better in my head than anywhere else. I would take some Oscar Peterson, John Coltrane,

Giant Steps and *My Favorite Things*. Stravinsky's *Rite of Spring*. Chopin's *Nocturnes*, even the simpler stuff. I would take one rhapsody by Liszt or piano concerto. I would take all of Beethoven's works except for *Missa Solemnis*, because if I was on a desert island I don't think I would spend the time getting tanned listening to *Missa Solemnis*. But I would certainly take all of his symphonies. I would probably bring some Jimi Hendrix, *Electric Ladyland* or something like that. Maybe I'd take the Sex Pistols, the first single they put out, to remind me the record industry was a world of extremes. I would take some Peter Gabriel; I would take *So*. I would take some Sting. I would take some world music, some African music and music from Brazil, China, Japan, Bali, wherever. I would take some chants. I would take the Bach *Mass in B Minor*. I would take *Heavy Weather* by Weather Report. Miles Davis, *My Funny Valentine* live with Tony Williams and Herbie Hancock. Led Zeppelin, I would take some selections. *Physical Graffiti* in its whole entirety. Crosby, Stills and Nash, their first record. Zappa, the last one he put out. The '71 Fillmore and I would take all of his later stuff, which has been coming out now on a regular basis. I would take that *Unbelievable* piano piece called ''Lucy's Sleeping'' for two pianos. It's a fantastic piece of music. Zappa's one of the greatest, if not the most influential composer of this century. I would take some other Yes stuff, maybe *Close to the Edge*. I love Yes's music. I would also take the *Refugee* album with me.

steve: I'd be tempted to take things that I really listen to a lot, but I might get tired of listening to them. There's one bit of music that means a lot to me and that's Jean-Pierre Rampal playing Bach's flute sonatas with harpsichord. I find that's something I really like to hear. I love flute music a lot, the flute's a fascinating instrument. There's an awful lot of things I like. I'm tempted to take a risk on something that I might be able to treat as a record for there, because if I was on a desert island I'd like to put a bundle of things away. There's things I'd have, but it sounds crazy thinking I'd take something there. I think I would like to take something that I'd played on.

chris: I'd take some Jimi Hendrix, maybe *Axis Bold as Love*. Stravinsky, *The Rite of Spring*.

I listen to radio. I like a lot of the new bands; the Soundgardens, the Pearl Jams . . . I think they're really good. I like Smashing Pumpkins a lot too. I do like quite a lot of what's out at the moment. The Cranberries. It doesn't surprise me anymore when they play a new band and I like it. There was a period, obviously, when, especially during the Glam/Heavy Metal period . . . ''Oh please. This is too much!'' A lot of those bands have completely died.

trevor rabin: In no particular order . . .

1. Leonard Bernstein conducting the New York Philharmonic doing the *1812 Overture*.
2. Ashkenazy playing the Rachmaninoff C minor.
3. The Paganini caprices performed by Heifitz.
4. Any Schoenberg.
5. *Apocalypse*, Mahavishnu Orchestra.
6. *Electric Ladyland*, Hendrix.
7. *Bookends*, Simon and Garfunkel.

8. The Bulgarian Choir.
9. Anything with Oscar Peterson. I love him—he's a tremendous player.
10. Rimsky-Korsakov, *Scheherazade* is one of my favorite pieces.
11. Antonio Carlos Jobim with Elis Regina did an album called *Elis and Tom*. A phenomenal record.

eddie: There wouldn't be any Yes on there, that's for sure! That's a really hard question to answer. There'd definitely be a lot of classical music. I like Beethoven and Holst. That kind of stuff just takes me away. I like the Police—I don't know . . . rock 'n' roll, been there—done it! Actually the only albums that I've produced that I would take with me are *True Stories* and *Just As I Thought* by David Sancious. It was so much fun putting those records together. . . . He's got the soul, he's got the feeling, and he's got all the chops and technique. And he's very humble—what a great guy.

rick (1993):

1. *Close to the Edge,* that LP was without a doubt one of the finest moments of Yes's career.
2. *All American Boy,* Rick Derringer.
3. Something from PFM and Barclay James Harvest. (YIS)

jon (1994): The only music that I buy now is world music, ancient Chinese music, South American salsa band music. I don't buy modern rock 'n' roll because there isn't that explosion anymore in terms of music prowess. (YM)

(1992): I know that I look at certain artists and I gravitate to their energy . . . Sibelius, Delius, Rickie Lee Jones. I love Sibelius. I think he's the greatest archetype of musical form that I can ever wish to understand. And I understand him more because I listen to him constantly. Frederick Delius I like very much. I mention these people again in the hopes that somebody will go listen to them, because they are great. It doesn't take an intellectual person to understand how great they are. One just needs to relax and enjoy them. (COTM)

A SELECT DISCOGRAPHY

JON ANDERSON

SOLO:
Olias of Sunhillow / Atlantic 1976
Song of Seven / Atlantic 1980
Animation / Atlantic 1982
Three Ships / Elektra 1985
In the City of Angels / CBS 1988
Deseo / Windham Hill 1994
Change We Must / Angel EMI 1994
Angels Embrace / Opio 1995
Toltec / Windham Hill 1996

WITH VANGELIS:
Short Stories / Polydor 1980
The Friends of Mr. Cairo / Polydor 1981
Private Collection / Polydor 1983
The Best of Jon And Vangelis / Polydor 1984
Page of Life / Arista 1991

ANDERSON BRUFORD WAKEMAN HOWE

Anderson Bruford Wakeman Howe / Arista 1989
An Evening of Yes Music Plus / Caroline 1994

PETER BANKS

SOLO:
Two Sides / Sovereign 1973
Instinct / Wildcat 1993
Self Contained / One Way Records 1995

WITH FLASH:
Flash / Sovereign 1972
Flash in the Can / Sovereign 1973
Out of Our Hands / Sovereign 1973
(The entire Peter Banks catalog is now available on One Way Records)

WITH OTHERS:
Tales from Yesterday / Magna Carta 1995

BILL BRUFORD

SOLO:
Feels Good to Me / Polydor 1978
One of a Kind / Polydor 1979
Gradually Going Tornado / Polydor 1980
The Bruford Tapes / E. G. Records 1979

WITH KING CRIMSON:
Lark's Tongues in Aspic / Atlantic 1973
Starless and Bible Black / Atlantic 1974
Red / Atlantic 1974
USA / Atlantic 1974
Discipline / Atlantic 1981
Beat / Atlantic 1982
Three of a Perfect Pair / Atlantic 1984
Thrak / Virgin 1995

WITH U.K.:
U.K. / Polydor 1978

WITH EARTHWORKS:
Earthworks / E. G. Records 1986
Dig / E. G. Records 1989
All Heaven Broke Loose / E. G. Records 1991
Stamping Ground, Live / Virgin 1994
(The entire Bill Bruford catalog is now available on Virgin / Caroline Records)

GEOFF DOWNES

SOLO:
The Light Program / Geffen 1987
Vox Humana / All At Once Records 1994

WITH THE BUGGLES:
The Age of Plastic / Island 1980
Adventures in Modern Recording / Carrere 1981

WITH ASIA:
Asia / Geffen 1982
Alpha / Geffen 1983

Astra / Geffen 1985
Then and Now / Geffen 1991
Aqua / Geffen 1992
Live in Moscow / Rhino 1992
Aria / Mayhem 1994

STEVE HOWE

SOLO:
Beginnings / Atlantic 1975
The Steve Howe Album / Atlantic 1979
Turbulence / Relativity 1991
The Grand Scheme of Things / Relativity 1993
Not Necessarily Acoustic / Caroline 1994
Mothballs / EMI 1995

WITH TOMORROW:
Tomorrow / Sire 1968

WITH BODAST:
Bodast / Cherry Red Records 1981

WITH ASIA:
Asia / Geffen 1982
Alpha / Geffen 1983
Then and Now / Geffen 1991
Aqua / Geffen 1992

WITH GTR:
GTR / Arista 1986

WITH OTHERS:
Billy Currie, Transportation / IRS 1988
Paul Sutin / Real Music 1989
Symphonic Music of Yes / RCA 1993
Tales from Yesterday / Magna Carta 1995

TREVOR HORN

WITH THE BUGGLES:
The Age of Plastic / Island 1980
Adventures in Modern Recording / Carrere 1981

TONY KAYE

WITH BADGER:
One Live Badger / Atlantic 1971
White Lady / Epic 1974

WITH DETECTIVE:
Detective / Swan Song 1977
It Takes One to Know One / Swan Song 1977
Live from Atlantic Studios / Swan Song 1978

WITH BADFINGER:
Say No More / Atlantic 1981

P A T R I C K   M O R A Z
SOLO:
The Story of i / Atlantic 1976
Out in the Sun / Import 1977
Patrick Moraz / Charisma 1978
Coexistence (with Syrinx) / Carrere 1980
Future Memories / Carrere 1980
Time Code / Passport 1984
Future Memories II / Passport 1985
Human Interface / Cinema 1987
Windows of Time / iSpirit 1994

WITH THE MOODY BLUES:
Long Distance Voyager / Threshold 1981
The Present / Threshold 1983
The Other Side of Life / Threshold 1986
Sur La Mer / Threshold 1988

WITH BILL BRUFORD:
Music for Piano and Drums / E. G. Records 1983
Flags / E. G. Records 1985

WITH OTHERS:
Mainhorse / Import 1971
Refugee / Charisma 1974
Tales From Yesterday / Magna Carta 1995

T R E V O R   R A B I N
SOLO:
Trevor Rabin / Chrysalis 1978
Face to Face / Chrysalis 1979
Wolf / Chrysalis 1981
Can't Look Away / Elektra 1989

WITH RABBITT:
Boys Will Be Boys / Capricorn 1976
A Croak and a Grunt in the Night / Capricorn 1977

AS A PRODUCER:
Chance / Manfred Mann's Earth Band / Warner Bros 1980

C H R I S   S Q U I R E
SOLO:
Fish Out of Water / Atlantic 1975

WITH OTHERS:
Euphoria / Magna Carta 1995

R I C K   W A K E M A N
SOLO:
The Six Wives of Henry The VIII / A&M 1973
Journey to the Centre Of The Earth / A&M 1974
Myths and Legends of King Arthur and the Knights of the Round Table / A&M 1975
Lisztomania / A&M 1975
No Earthly Connection / A&M 1976
White Rock / A&M 1977
Criminal Record / A&M 1977
Rhapsodies / A&M 1979
1984 / Charisma 1981
Rock 'n' Roll Prophet / Moon 1982
G'ole / Charisma 1982
The Burning / Varese Sarabande 1982
Cost of Living / Charisma 1983
Silent Nights / TGB 1985
Live at the Hammersmith / TGB 1985
Beyond the Planets / Telstar 1985
Country Airs / Coda 1986
Crimes of Passion / President 1986
The Gospels / Stylus 1987
The Family Album / President 1987
A Suite of Gods / President 1987
Time Machine / President 1988
Zodiaque / President 1988
Sea Airs / President 1989
In the Beginning / Asaph 1990
Night Airs / President 1991
Black Knights at the Court of Ferdinand IV / Ambient 1991
Phantom Power / Ambient 1991
Aspirant Sunset / Ambient 1991
Aspirant Sunrise / Ambient 1991
Aspirant Shadows / Ambient 1991
Suntrilogy / Ambient 1991
Soft Sword / Rio Digital 1991

2000 AD into the Future / Ambient 1991
African Bach / Quattro 1991
The Private Collection / Ambient 1991
The Classical Connection / Ambient 1993
The Heritage Suite / President 1993
Wakeman with Wakeman / President 1993
Prayers / Word UK 1993
No Expense Spared / President 1993
Wakeman with Wakeman Live, The Official Bootleg / President 1994
Live on the Test / 1994
Almost Live in Europe / Griffin 1995

WITH THE STRAWBS:
Just a Collection of Antiques And Curios / A&M 1970
From the Witchwood / A&M 1971

ALAN WHITE

SOLO:
Ramshackled / Atlantic 1976

WITH THE PLASTIC ONO BAND:
Live Peace in Toronto / Apple 1970
Imagine / Apple 1971
Sometime in NYC / Apple 1972

WITH GEORGE HARRISON:
All Things Must Pass / Apple 1970

WITH JOHNNY HARRIS:
All To Bring You Morning / Warner Bros 1973

WITH EDDIE HARRIS:
E. H. in U.K. / Atlantic 1974

YES

Yes / Atlantic 1969
Time and a Word / Atlantic 1970
The Yes Album / Atlantic 1971
Fragile / Atlantic 1972
Close to the Edge / Atlantic 1972
Yessongs / Atlantic 1973
Tales from Topographic Oceans / Atlantic 1974
Relayer / Atlantic 1974
Yesterdays / Atlantic 1975
Going for the One / Atlantic 1977
Tormato / Atlantic 1978
Drama / Atlantic 1980
Yesshows / Atlantic 1980
Classic Yes / Atlantic 1982
90125 / Atlantic 1983
9012LIVE / Atlantic 1985
Big Generator / Atlantic 1987
Union / Arista 1991
Yesyears / Atlantic 1991
Yesstory / Atlantic 1991
Highlights: The Very Best Of Yes / Atlantic 1993
Talk / Victory 1994

SOURCES

I am gratefully indebted to the following publications for material used in my book. I highly recommend any of them for your own Yes-quest.

BOOKS
British Rock Guitar (BRG) By Dan Hedges
Music Producers (M) From the editors of *Mix* magazine
Rick Wakeman: The Caped Crusader (RWCC) By Dan Wooding
The Steve Howe Guitar Collection (SHGC) By Steve Howe
Steve Howe Guitar Pieces (SHGP) By Mick Barker and Steve Howe
Yes: The Authorized Biography (YAB) By Dan Hedges

MAGAZINES
BAM (BAM)
Bass Player (BP) (Chris Squire Interview, November 1994)
Beat Magazine (BTM)
Children of the Moon (COTM)

Circus (C) (Special thanks to Jerry Rothberg)

Connecting Link (CL) (excerpted with permission from Connecting Link C/O 9392 Whit-neyville S.E., Alto, MI 49302–9694 (616) 891–0410)

Creem Magazine (CM)

Downbeat (DB)

Gig (GIG)

Guitar for the Practicing Musician (G) (published by Cherry Lane Music; special thanks to Harvey Newquist and Chris Gentry)

August 1986, "GTR Stands for Guitar" by John Stix

Winter 1987, "Steve Howe Virtuoso of the Rock Guitar" by John Stix

September 1989, "Steve Howe No Maybes" by John Stix

Guitar Player (GP) (special thanks to Peggi Clapham)

(Steve Howe Interview, May 1978)

Guitar School (GS) (special thanks to Brad Tolinsky)

Guitar Shop (GTRSP) (special thanks to Harvey Newquist and Chris Gentry)

Summer 1994, New Beginnings (Steve Howe) by Pete Prown

The Guitar Magazine, UK (GTM) (special thanks to Paul Tingen)

Guitar World (GW) (special thanks to Brad Tolinsky)

Hit Parader (HP)

Keyboard (K)

(Rick Wakeman Interview, March/April 1976)

(Rick Wakeman Interview, February 1979)

(Geoff Downes Interview, March 1981)

(Patrick Moraz Interview, November 1981)

(Geoff Downes Interview, November 1983)

(Rick Wakeman Interview, September 1989)

(Patrick Moraz Interview, May 1991)

(Wakeman/Kaye Interview, August 1991)

(Trevor Rabin Interview, June 1994)

Keyboard World (KW)

Macrobiotics Today (MT) (material used by the kind permission of The George Ohsawa Macrobiotic Foundation, 1999 Myers Street, Oroville, CA 95966)

Melody Maker (MM) (special thanks to Maria Jefferis)

Modern Drummer (MD) (reprinted by permission of Modern Drummer, Cedar Grove, NJ; special thanks to Bill Miller)

Modern Hi-Fi & Stereo Guide (MHF)

Modern Recording and Music (MR)

Musician (MN)

Music News Network (MNN) (special thanks to Christine Holz and Lisa Mikita)

The Music Press (TMP)

Music Technology (MAT)

Notes from the Edge (NFTE) (The Yes Internet Source)

#65: The Alan White Interview, © 1993 Mike Tiano. All rights reserved.

#80: The Steve Howe Interview, © 1993 Mike Tiano. All rights reserved.

#88: The Steve Howe Interview, © 1994 Mike Tiano. All rights reserved.

#104: The Chris Squire Interview, © 1994 Mike Tiano. All rights reserved.

#124: The Steve Howe Interview, © 1995 Mike Tiano. All rights reserved.

#125: The Steve Howe Interview, © 1995 Mike Tiano. All rights reserved.

Phonograph Record (PR)

Q Magazine (Q)

Record Review (RR)

Relayer (R) (special thanks to Tanya Coad)

The Revealing (TR) (special thanks to Ian Hartley and Paul Williams)

Rolling Stone (RS)

"Yes: The Band That Stays Healthy, Plays Healthy" by Cameron Crowe. From *RS*, June 7, 1973. By Straight Arrow Publishers, Inc. 1973. All Rights Reserved. Reprinted by Permission.

"Rick Wakeman Brings the Brew Back to Yes" by Billy Altman. From *RS*, October 6, 1977. By Straight Arrow Publishers, Inc. 1977. All Rights Reserved. Reprinted by Permission.

Seconds (S) (courtesy of *Seconds* magazine, by Steven Blush)

Song Talk (ST)

Sounds (SDS)

Trouser Press (TP)

Vegetarian Times (VT)

Vintage Guitar Magazine (VG)

Wonderous Stories (WS) (special thanks to Suzanne Cerquone)

Yes Information Service (YIS) (special thanks to Nic Caciappo)

Yes Magazine (YM) (special thanks to Glenn and Doug Gottlieb)

Credits correspond to text in order in which they appear:

Yes Magazine, Volume 4 Number 2. © Copyright 1992 *Yes Magazine*/Douglas Gottlieb & Glenn Gottlieb. All rights reserved. Used by permission.

Yes Magazine, Volume 4 Number 2. © Copyright 1992 *Yes Magazine*/Douglas Gottlieb & Glenn Gottlieb. All rights reserved. Used by permission.

Yes Magazine, Volume 2 Number 1. © Copyright 1989 *Yes Magazine*/Douglas Gottlieb & Glenn Gottlieb. All rights reserved. Used by permission.

Yes Magazine, Volume 4 Number 3. © Copyright 1993 *Yes Magazine*/Douglas Gottlieb & Glenn Gottlieb. All rights reserved. Used by permission.

Yes Magazine, Volume 5 Number 2. © Copyright 1994 *Yes Magazine*/Douglas Gottlieb & Glenn Gottlieb. All rights reserved. Used by permission.

Yes Magazine, Volume 5 Number 2. © Copyright 1994 *Yes Magazine*/Douglas Gottlieb & Glenn Gottlieb. All rights reserved. Used by permission.

Yes Magazine, Volume 1 Number 3. © Copyright 1988 *Yes Magazine*/Douglas Gottlieb & Glenn Gottlieb. All rights reserved. Used by permission.

Yes Magazine, Volume 2 Number 1. © Copyright 1989 *Yes Magazine*/Douglas Gottlieb & Glenn Gottlieb. All rights reserved. Used by permission.

Yes Magazine, Volume 4 Number 2. © Copyright 1992 *Yes Magazine*/Douglas Gottlieb & Glenn Gottlieb. All rights reserved. Used by permission.

Yes Magazine, Volume 2 Number 1. © Copyright 1989 *Yes Magazine*/Douglas Gottlieb & Glenn Gottlieb. All rights reserved. Used by permission.

Yes Magazine, Volume 2 Number 1. © Copyright 1989 *Yes Magazine*/Douglas Gottlieb & Glenn Gottlieb. All rights reserved. Used by permission.

Yes Magazine, Volume 5 Number 1. © Copyright 1993 *Yes Magazine*/Douglas Gottlieb & Glenn Gottlieb. All rights reserved. Used by permission.

Yes Magazine, Volume 4 Number 2. © Copyright 1992 *Yes Magazine*/Douglas Gottlieb & Glenn Gottlieb. All rights reserved. Used by permission.

Yes Magazine, Volume 5 Number 2. © Copyright 1994 *Yes Magazine*/Douglas Gottlieb & Glenn Gottlieb. All rights reserved. Used by permission.

Yes Magazine, Volume 5 Number 2. © Copyright 1994 *Yes Magazine*/Douglas Gottlieb & Glenn Gottlieb. All rights reserved. Used by permission.

Yes Magazine, Volume 5 Number 2. © Copyright 1994 *Yes Magazine*/Douglas Gottlieb & Glenn Gottlieb. All rights reserved. Used by permission.

RADIO SHOWS
Ed Sciaky Interviews (ES)
Inner-view With Chris Squire (I)
In The Studio (ITS) (special thanks to Redbeard)
The World Premiere Of Union (UP) (special thanks to Redbeard)
The World Premiere of Talk (TPRS) (special thanks to Bob Coburn)
   (Thank you to Mark Felsot and The Album Network for use of these broadcasts)
Yes Holiday Special (YHS)
Yes Music: An Evening With Jon Anderson (YMRS)

VIDEOS
Anderson Bruford Wakeman Howe (Pay Per View) (ABWH)
Bruford and the Beat (BB) (Ken Klompuss and Steve Apicella, producers)
Sounding Out Yes BBC (SOY)
Star Licks Presents Chris Squire (CSV)
Yes: Rockumentary (MTV)
Yes: Greatest Video Hits (YGVH)
Yesyears (YY) (special thanks to Jodi Heller, courtesy of Warner Vision Entertainment)
Yestival '94 (YV) (Christine Holz / Lisa Mikita)

ALL OTHER QUOTES ARE FROM TIM MORSE INTERVIEWS (TMI)

FAN PUBLICATIONS

CLOSE TO YES
62 1311 HH ALMERE
THE NETHERLANDS

MUSIC NEWS NETWORK
P.O. BOX 21531
TAMPA, FL 33622-1531

NOTES FROM THE EDGE
(THE INTERNET YES SOURCE)
WEB SITE:
HTTP://WWW. NFTE.ORG/
E-MAIL:
NFTE@SOL.CMS.UNCWIL.EDU
P.O. BOX 2721
REDMOND, WA 98073-2721

OPIO FOUNDATION
P.O. BOX 15051
WILMINGTON, NC 28412

THE REVEALING
12 W. ACRE, CHURCH GRESLEY
SWADLINCOTE, DERBYSHIRE
DE11 9RW ENGLAND

RICK WAKEMAN COMMUNICA-
TION CENTRE
BAJONOR HOUSE
2 BRIDGE STREET
PEEL, ISLE OF MAN
ENGLAND

STEVE HOWE APPRECIATION
   SOCIETY
C/O PAM BAY
154 HICKS FARM RISE
HIGH WYCOMBE, BUCKS
HP13 7SG ENGLAND

TOPOGRAPHIC SOUNDS
APARTADO DECORREOS
40.080
28080 MADRID, SPAIN

YES FAMILY FAN CLUB
2F-1 SAIKISOU
3-159 YAMAMOTOCHO

NAKAKU, YOKOHAMA
KANAGAWA 231 JAPAN

YES INFORMATION SERVICE
C/O BEAT MUSIC, NIC CACIAPPO
2221 MCHENRY AVE, SUITE E
MODESTO, CA 95350

YES MAGAZINE
12 CHELSEA PLACE
DIX HILLS, NY 11746

YES MUSIC CIRCLE
P.O. BOX 310
GUILDFORD, SURREY
GU2 5WH ENGLAND

The *90125* lineup on a shoot for the Talk tour, 1994.
CAROLINE GREYSHOCK, COURTESY VICTORY/EAST END MANAGEMENT